A
MARTYR'S FAITH
in a
FAITHLESS WORLD

Bryan Wolfmueller

CONCORDIA PUBLISHING HOUSE · SAINT LOUIS

Concordia
Publishing House

Founded in 1869 as the publishing arm of The Lutheran
Church—Missouri Synod, Concordia Publishing House gives
all glory to God for the blessing of 150 years of opportunities
to provide resources that are faithful to the Holy Scriptures
and the Lutheran Confessions.

Published by Concordia Publishing House
3558 S. Jefferson Ave., St. Louis, MO 63118-3968
1-800-325-3040 • cph.org

Manufactured in the United States of America

Library of Congress Cataloging-in-Publication Data

Names: Wolfmueller, Bryan, author.

Title: A martyr's faith in a faithless world / C. Bryan Wolfmueller.

Description: Saint Louis : Concordia Publishing House, 2019.

Identifiers: LCCN 2019008284 (print) | LCCN 2019021803 (ebook) | ISBN
9780758662507 | ISBN 9780758662491

Subjects: LCSH: Lutheran Church. | Lutheran Church--Doctrines. | Christian
saints. | Christian life--Lutheran authors.

Classification: LCC BX8065.3 (ebook) | LCC BX8065.3 .W655 2019 (print) | DDC
230/.41--dc23

LC record available at https://lccn.loc.gov/2019008284

1   2   3   4   5   6   7   8   9   10   28   27   26   25   24   23   22   21   20   19

To Hannah, Andrew, Daniel, and Isaac

*With the prayer and confidence that
your hearts will remain the good dirt.*

For I am already being poured out as a drink offering,

and the time of my departure has come.

I have fought the good fight,

I have finished the race,

I have kept the faith.

*Henceforth there is laid up for me the
crown of righteousness,*

which the Lord, the righteous judge,

will award to me on that day,

and not only to me

but also to all who have loved His appearing.

2 Timothy 4:6–8

Contents

PART 4: IN THE WEEDS

PART 5: GOOD DIRT

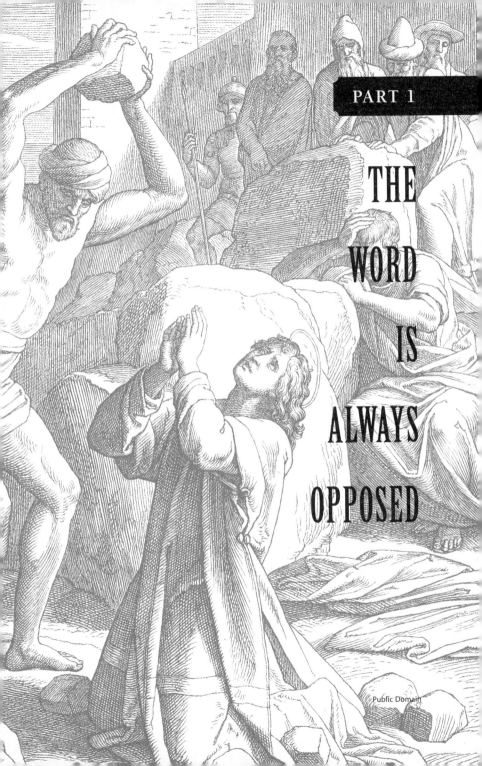

PART 1

THE
WORD
IS
ALWAYS
OPPOSED

ST. STEPHEN: MARTYR. HERO.
AD 34, JERUSALEM.
ACTS 6–7

Three and a half years after the ascension of Jesus, the Church in Jerusalem was continuing to grow. New disciples were baptized and added to the number of Christians, and the administrative burdens were adding up.

The Twelve elected seven deacons to help care for the widows. Stephen was one of the chosen. He was "full of faith and of the Holy Spirit" (6:5) and was doing great wonders.

One synagogue in Jerusalem was particularly troubled by Stephen's teaching. Some of the men stood against Stephen and tried to refute him, but they were unable to do so. Having failed, they started a rumor that Stephen was preaching against Moses and speaking blasphemies against God. They agitated against Stephen based on this rumor, so Stephen was brought before the Sanhedrin, where false witnesses repeated the rumors.

Standing in front of the same council that condemned Jesus to be crucified, Stephen was also falsely accused. But he was unfazed. Even the council noted that "his face was like the face of an angel" (6:15).

"Are these things so?" the high priests demanded (7:1).

Stephen's answer is a sermon that weaves together the two great themes of the Old Testament: the grace of God and the rebellion of the people. He defended himself a little. He accused them a lot. It turned out that the real rejecters of Moses and the true blasphemers of God were those who crucified Jesus. "You stiff-necked people," he concluded, without a touch of fear, "uncircumcised in heart and ears, you always resist the Holy Spirit. As your fathers did, so do you. Which of the prophets did your fathers not persecute? And they killed those who announced beforehand the coming of the Righteous One, whom you have now betrayed and murdered, you who received the law as delivered by angels and did not keep it" (7:51–53).

The council members were enraged. They ground their teeth at him. But Stephen, looking up to heaven, was given a vision of the throne room of God. He saw the glory of God. "Behold," he said, "I see the heavens opened, and the Son of Man standing at the right hand of God" (7:56).

They shouted. They covered their ears. They rushed together at him. They grabbed Stephen, dragged him outside the city walls, and with fury stoned him. "Lord Jesus, receive my spirit" (7:59). Stephen was knocked to his knees, and with his dying breath he prayed for his murderers. "Lord, do not hold this sin against them" (7:60).

Stephen: Martyr. Hero.

We'll meet in the resurrection.

1

Christians Need Heroes

*We are surrounded by so
great a cloud of witnesses.*

(HEBREWS 12:1)

I heard someone say, "You can learn all you need to know about a
person if you know who their heroes are." They were on to something.
We live in the shadow of our heroes. We look up to them. We try to live
like them. Our heroes encourage us and inspire us.

If they are good heroes, they encourage us to trust God and believe
His promises in the midst of all sorts of trouble.

Christians need heroes who remind us of God's mercy. We see in
their lives how God forgives sinners and saves the ungodly. Heroes such
as David and Paul remind us that the Lord can forgive murder, adultery,
and raging against the Church.

Christians need heroes who remind us to thank God for all His gifts
and that He raised up great men and women before us to teach us and
bless us. Our heroes Moses and Matthew remind us to give thanks to
God for their writings, for their Spirit-inspired wisdom recorded in the
Scriptures for us.

Christians need heroes who can stand as examples, especially when
the Lord gives us their same vocations and callings. Mary and Joseph are
heroes for parents. Stephen is a hero for preachers. David is a hero for

rulers. And all the Christian heroes are our examples in faith and love, in prayer and joy, in patience, in suffering, and in death.

Christians need heroes who pray. Christians need heroes who serve. Christians need heroes who suffer with patience.

Christians need heroes who die.

The Christian hero is not the person who has obtained all that he or she desires in this life. Our heroes are not those who have gained the entire world but lost their soul. Our heroes are not those who have achieved a great degree of worldly success or notoriety. Our heroes are those who have fought the good fight and kept the faith, and who have finished the race. Our heroes are those who have stood against the wiles of the devil, who have stood against the wild beasts (see 1 Corinthians 15:32) of the world and the flesh. And having stood, our heroes are those who have died the blessed death.

Hebrews 11 puts these heroes before us and gives us clarity as to why they are heroes. Abel, Enoch, and Noah are *not* our heroes because they experienced all this world had to offer. Abraham and Sarah are *not* our heroes because they lived the life of their dreams. Jacob, Joseph, and Moses are *not* our heroes because of their fame or fortune. They are our heroes because they trusted in God. They are our heroes because they believed in the things God promised, things that they did not live to see. They never let go of these promises—not in life, in sorrow, in suffering, not even in death.

> **These all died in faith, not having received the things promised, but having seen them and greeted them from afar, and having acknowledged that they were strangers and exiles on the earth.** (HEBREWS 11:13)

Dear Christian, your heroes are strangers, wanderers, exiles on earth. Your heroes have a discontent with this world, knowing that there is something better. They have their eyes on the resurrection, the life and the world to come. They have their hearts set on the new heaven and the new earth where righteousness lives (see 2 Peter 3:13).

> But as it is, they desire a better country, that is, a heavenly one. Therefore God is not ashamed to be called their God, for He has prepared for them a city. (HEBREWS 11:16)

The Bible puts before us heroes who lived by faith and not by sight (2 Corinthians 5:7). Faith means trusting promises. Christians walk by the words and promises of God. The goal of each Christian is to make it to the end of life still trusting in those promises. And this is the victory: to trust the promises of God through death.

> And what more shall I say? For time would fail me to tell of Gideon, Barak, Samson, Jephthah, of David and Samuel and the prophets—who through faith conquered kingdoms, enforced justice, obtained promises, stopped the mouths of lions, quenched the power of fire, escaped the edge of the sword, were made strong out of weakness, became mighty in war, put foreign armies to flight. Women received back their dead by resurrection. Some were tortured, refusing to accept release, so that they might rise again to a better life. Others suffered mocking and flogging, and even chains and imprisonment. They were stoned, they were sawn in two, they were killed with the sword. They went about in skins of sheep and goats, destitute, afflicted, mistreated—of whom the world was not worthy—wandering about in deserts and mountains, and in dens and caves of the earth. And all these, though commended through their faith, did not receive what was promised, since God had provided something better for us, that apart from us they should not be made perfect. (HEBREWS 11:32–40)

Do you see the suffering? Do you see the affliction? Do you see the dying? These are not the heroes in the movies. They are not the kind of people whom the world wants to follow. To do so means to follow them into death. These heroes are the great cloud of witnesses (see Hebrews 12:1) who are put before the Christian to encourage and enliven faith. These are the heroes God sets before us.

Consider this. If the goal that God has for us is to die in the faith, then the goal the devil has in mind for us is to put our faith to death. The devil does not want us to believe and trust in God. He does not want us to have the promise of the forgiveness of sins. He does not want us to attain the resurrection of the dead and life eternal. He does not rest in his attempts to overthrow us.

One of the devil's tactics is to provide alternative heroes. Life, success, peace, comfort, fame, whatever—the devil's heroes win a different fight. They finish a different race. They carry their accomplishments in this world as victory. The Christian heroes carry the cross.

This only makes sense.

Our true and ultimate hero, our champion and chief contender, is Jesus. Jesus, who died. Jesus, who took upon Himself flesh and blood so that He could die (see Hebrews 2:14–15). Jesus, the immortal God who bound Himself to our sin, our shame, even our death to save us.

We have a God who bleeds. We have a God who suffers. We have a God who was hated by the world. We have a God who had a tomb. We have Jesus, who says with His dying breath, "It is finished" (John 19:30).

"It is finished."

There is so much in that little sermon of Jesus. There are so many things that are finished.

The work of salvation, which He came to accomplish: finished.

The sacrifice, the substitutionary atonement for the sins of humanity: finished.

The war between heaven and earth: finished.

The mad and endless attempts for us to win our own salvation: finished.

The way from death to life for sinners: finished.

The anguish of the cross, the suffering of God's wrath in our place: finished.

The earthly work and life of Jesus: finished.

The death of Jesus is everything for us. It is our hope and life. It is our doctrine. It is our preaching. And it is even our example. Jesus shows us our finish line.

A lot of things can be accomplished in this life—a lot of things to do and see, to say and build, a lot of delight and suffering. But when it is all over and our last hour comes, only one thing matters: faith when dying. Jesus says, "If anyone would come after Me, let him deny himself and take up his cross and follow Me" (Matthew 16:24). Faith is following Jesus through death to life. But first through death.

This, I think, is why Christians have always considered the martyrs to be heroes. The martyrs are those who died for their faith. They endured all sorts of terrible afflictions and abuse because they confessed Christ. They preached with their lives, their lips, and their blood. In the lives and deaths of the martyrs, we see the devil's rage on full display, and we see that his rage comes to nothing—that he is impotent and overcome by the blood of the Lamb and the word of testimony of those who did not love their lives unto death (Revelation 12:11).

The martyrs remind us that there is nothing that the devil can do to us. The martyrs remind us that death is nothing to fear. The martyrs preach to us the victory of the death of Jesus. The martyrs show us how to die. The martyrs encourage us as we are finishing our race; they are cheering for us and reminding us what—or better, who—is at the finish line waiting for us. Jesus stands, waiting for us.

> **Therefore, since we are surrounded by so great a cloud of witnesses, let us also lay aside every weight, and sin which clings so closely, and let us run with endurance the race that is set before us, looking to Jesus, the founder and perfecter of our faith.** (HEBREWS 12:1–2)

2

The Planted Word

Receive with meekness the implanted word,
which is able to save your souls.

(JAMES 1:21)

A sower went out to sow.

(MATTHEW 13:3)

Jesus is painting a picture for us, and we want to see it. Winter has ended. The sun warms the ground. It's planting season. The farmer gathers the seed out of the barn, puts the satchel over his shoulder, and goes out to sow. His hand reaches into the bag, grabs a pile of seed, and flings it with gladness and hope into the soil.

The seed is sown in hope. The sower hopes that the seed will find a place, will take root, and will grow into a bountiful harvest. He sings and scatters and walks up and down his field, imagining the joy of the harvest a few months away.

Alas, not every seed matures. Not every seed grows into a plant. Some don't make it.

This gets us closer to what Jesus wants us to know. It's dangerous for the seed.

> And as he sowed, some seeds fell along the path, and the
> birds came and devoured them. Other seeds fell on rocky
> ground, where they did not have much soil, and immedi-
> ately they sprang up, since they had no depth of soil, but
> when the sun rose they were scorched. And since they had
> no root, they withered away. Other seeds fell among thorns,
> and the thorns grew up and choked them. (MATTHEW 13:4–7)

We can see it in our imagination as Jesus continues to paint the picture. Some of the seed falls onto the hard-packed dirt path, and the sparrows flutter around, snatching up the seed. The seed barely touches the ground before it is devoured.

Other seed falls in among the rocks. We have to imagine this with time-lapse: the plants grow up quickly, quicker even than the seed that falls in the good ground. They look healthy and robust, the best plants of all. But when the heat of midsummer comes, these plants lack the needed deep roots, and they wither and die.

Still other seed falls among the weeds and thorns on the edge of the field. These seeds also grow into little plants, but then the thorns surround them and choke them out. These also die.

Gloomy.

There is high drama in this field. The sower has sent out all this seed in the expectation of the harvest, but these seeds fail. None come to the intended end. This is the warning and wisdom of this parable: the seed is opposed. The seed is in danger. The seed is attacked from every side, and often overcome.

Jesus, though, does not end there. He has one more scene for us to see. Jesus brings us through the summer to the fall, to the harvest. The fields are full, and the sower now comes to reap the harvest.

> Other seeds fell on good soil and produced grain, some
> a hundredfold, some sixty, some thirty. (MATTHEW 13:8)

There is hope. There is a harvest. Not every seed will make it, but the sower does not sow in vain. At the end, there is life and abundance. This is the picture that Jesus gives us, but what does it mean?

The disciples wondered the same thing, and we can thank God that Jesus told them.

The seed is the Word of God: the preaching of the death and resurrection of Jesus. The soils are the ears and hearts of sinners.

Beginning with the seed that falls on the path, Jesus explains:

> **When anyone hears the word of the kingdom and does not understand it, the evil one comes and snatches away what has been sown in his heart. This is what was sown along the path.** (MATTHEW 13:19)

The evil one is the devil. He stands opposed to the Word of God from the very beginning. Like the birds on the sidewalk, the devil and the demons are fluttering around the preaching of the Word, ready to snatch it away before it takes root.

Jesus continues to the seed in the rocks:

> **As for what was sown on rocky ground, this is the one who hears the word and immediately receives it with joy, yet he has no root in himself, but endures for a while, and when tribulation or persecution arises on account of the word, immediately he falls away.** (MATTHEW 13:20–21)

Here are Christians with tiny little roots. When trouble comes, their faith dries up and withers away. Trouble will come. "In the world you will have tribulation" (John 16:33). Like the scorching sun on rootless plants, tribulation wreaks havoc on the Christian with shallow convictions.

The third group of seeds falls among the weeds and thorns. Jesus explains:

> **As for what was sown among thorns, this is the one who hears the word, but the cares of the world and the deceitfulness of riches choke the word, and it proves unfruitful.** (MATTHEW 13:22)

Cares, riches, the pleasures of this world are a danger to the seed, a danger to the Christian. Like weeds that grow up around a tender plant, the cares of this world grow up around our faith and choke it out. It isn't only bad times that attack our faith. The devil also uses good times and good things to cause our faith to wilt and diminish until nothing is left.

Jesus, with this parable, is outlining the three great dangers to the Christian faith and the preaching of the Word: the devil, the world, and our sinful flesh. These three enemies stand opposed to us and the eternal life that the Lord desires to harvest in us on the Last Day. These enemies are ever-present, subtle, and dangerous. But these enemies and the disasters they bring don't have the last word.

This parable of the sower is a parable of warning, but it ends with triumph—the seeds that fall in the good ground. With these, the sower finds the expected harvest.

> **As for what was sown on good soil, this is the one who hears the word and understands it. He indeed bears fruit and yields, in one case a hundredfold, in another sixty, and in another thirty.** (MATTHEW 13:23)

This is the end that Jesus is after. This is why He warns us about the dangers opposing our faith. And it's why I'm writing this book.

Every word that marches out of the Lord's mouth goes out to bless and bring forth life.

But every word that marches out of God's mouth is opposed. God's Word has enemies. The devil, the world, and our sinful flesh are its constant opponents.

The devil rages against the Word. The devil hates life. The devil hates what is good. The devil hates God's wisdom and kindness. The devil hates God. The devil hates the Word of God. He rages against it with fury.

The world is set against God. It wants its own rule. It loves the darkness and not the light. It cowers at the light of the Word.

The sinful flesh sniffs after the bread crumbs of desire, following them to death. It is blinded to the joy, beauty, and wisdom of God. Its mind is set on earthly things, and God's Word gets in the way of its pursuits.

The seed will always have birds, weeds, and shallow roots to contend with. The Christian's faith will always face opposition. But there is always help. "God is my helper" (Psalm 54:4). Jesus is our Savior.

We will, in the chapters to come, consider the attacks of the devil, the assaults of the world, and the fights of the sinful flesh, and see what strength, confidence, and comfort the Lord offers us for the fray. The Scriptures don't simply warn us about the dangers that face our faith, they also equip us for the fight. They expose the tactics of the devil, the world, and our flesh and give us all that we need to withstand the assault and, on the Last Day, stand with confidence in the Lord's life.

This is a martyr's faith in this faithless world. It is a pilgrim's faith that wanders with an eye on the dawning glory. It is the Christian faith that knows that our glory is hidden in Christ, waiting to be revealed on the Last Day.

The Word is opposed

3

Jesus Loves Me, This I Know

In this is love, not that we have loved God
but that He loved us and sent His Son
to be the propitiation for our sins.

(1 JOHN 4:10)

First, before all else, we want to know what the "seed of the Word" is. What is the preaching that yields the fruit of eternal life? What is the Bible all about?

The Bible is a love story.

God is love. You are the beloved.

This is particularly astonishing when we consider how unlovely and how unlovable we are.

The Bible tells us about this in the story of our rebellion. It unfolds the depth of our wretchedness. It tells the history of our first parents, Adam and Eve, who took hold of and ate the only thing in the world marked with the sign "Do not eat!—God."

That disobedience was death, and that disobedience and death continues in us. We are born in a state of rebellion against God, enemies of His kingdom. We deserve His rejection. We deserve His anger.

But God doesn't give us what we deserve. We get, instead, His love.

The love of God is much more than a feeling and affection. Because we are in a state of rebellion, God's love is a rescuing love. God's love is a seeking love. It is a bleeding and dying love. His love has work to do: work to make you right with Him, work to cover your rebellion.

This is why Jesus was born. The very Son of God became a human so that He could later be found bleeding and dying on a Roman cross: God forsaken by God for you.

Never was there love like this. Never was such a sacrifice made in all the history of history.

God took upon Himself the form of man—your humanity—so that He might dress Himself in your rebellion and take the punishment that you deserve, all so that you could live forever with Him. That really happened. No matter what else happens next, this matters most: the death of Jesus is the most significant event in the history of the world, and it is the most significant event in the history of your life (and in your death). The cross of Jesus is the most important thing to know, to believe, and to understand.

All of the great love stories of the Bible are the echoes and reverberations, mirroring or growing out of, the great love story of God and that cross, that death, that blood shed for you. That Jesus—truly and fully God and truly and fully man—your God, in your place, suffering, dying because He loves you.

The apostle John says it like this: "In this is love, not that we have loved God but that He loved us and sent His Son to be the propitiation for our sins" (1 John 4:10). John was copying Jesus, who said a few years earlier, "God so loved the world, that He gave His only Son, that whoever believes in Him should not perish but have eternal life" (John 3:16).

"Jesus loves me, this I know, for the Bible tells me so."

It is the simple truth we teach the children, but it is also the confession on the martyrs' lips as they go to die. "Jesus loves me." This is the foundational truth of the Bible, the bedrock of our faith, and it is also the height of our wisdom.

While our focus is on Christian maturity, how to have a martyr's faith in a faithless world, this does *not* mean moving beyond this simple truth.

So many books on discipleship and Christian maturity want to go beyond the Gospel, beyond the cross, beyond the simple truth, beyond the faith of a child. "The Gospel for the unbeliever; the Law for the believer" seems to be the motto of the day. Rather, let's do the opposite! Let's consider together how it is that God can love us sinners. Let's meditate on the mysteries of God as our Brother and our Friend. Let's fix our minds and our hearts on Jesus, who is both the author and finisher, the beginning and the end, of our faith.

Christian maturity is comprised of this: knowing the love of God in Christ and living in that love.

This is how Paul saw it. In a mysterious, surprising, and delightful text, Paul tells the Ephesian Christians what he prays for them—that they would know what is unknowable! Here's how he says it:

> [I pray] that Christ may dwell in your hearts through faith—that you, being rooted and grounded in love, may have strength to comprehend with all the saints what is the breadth and length and height and depth, and *to know the love of Christ that surpasses knowledge*, that you may be filled with all the fullness of God. (EPHESIANS 3:17–19)

Paul knows that it is impossible for our weak and rebellious minds to know the love of Christ. Still he prays that we would know the unknowable. This is the mystery of the Christian faith. We know what cannot be known, what cannot be comprehended:

That Jesus loves us.

That God has died for us.

That the Creator is our Rescuer and our Friend.

That He lives with us now, and we will live with Him forever.

Gospel gives power + desire to do good works (Christian living) (fruit)

4

The Bible Is Not (Only) a Children's Book

But I, brothers, could not address you as spiritual
people, but as people of the flesh, as infants in Christ.
I fed you with milk, not solid food, for you were
not ready for it. And even now you are not yet ready,
for you are still of the flesh.

(1 CORINTHIANS 3:1–3)

When I was a child, I spoke like a child, I thought
like a child, I reasoned like a child. When I became
a man, I gave up childish ways.

(1 CORINTHIANS 13:11)

When we learned to read, we started with the simplest things. We first learned our ABCs. We learned to write the letters and then our names. We were given books with big pictures and simple words. As we became better readers, things grew more complex. Sentences became paragraphs, which became chapter books. Not just the grammar but the ideas became more complex; the themes became nuanced and serious. Children's book are, well, childish. We grow out of them. You wouldn't read *Curious George* in a college lit class, and you wouldn't give *Hamlet* to a first grader.

But we *do* put the Bible in the hands of children, and this causes a problem. We are tempted to think of the Bible as a children's book.

We fill the imaginations of children with felt-board people and places. There is smiling Noah petting the smiling giraffe. There is King David (looking like he's twelve years old) waving a little sword at the friendly looking Goliath. There is Jesus, riding comfortably on the back of a smiling donkey into Jerusalem, a city that consists of three awkwardly placed square homes on top of a hill. Here is a nice book with nice people in nice places with a lot of happy endings. Everything is soft, every edge is rounded, all the grass is green, every story has a moral, and, as far as our imagination is concerned, Jesus is a cartoon.

Please don't misunderstand. We most certainly should teach Bible stories to our children. But we have to recognize the danger that if we think of the Bible as a children's book, then we will tend to put it away when we become adults. If the Bible is a cartoon, then we'll stop reading it about the time we stop watching cartoons. We will think that we've grown out of it.

The Bible is not a children's book.

It is full of smoldering grit.

It is the history of real people, sinful people, with real hurts and dreams, passion and fear. The cities are crowded; the plots are complicated; the motivations are complex. And it always surprises.

It is important, as we mature in Christ, that we mature in our understanding of the Bible, that we begin to read it as adults and engage with it as adults. Here are a few tips and suggestions:

1. SMELL THE TEXT.

A few years back a friend and younger pastor asked for preaching advice, and this is what I told him: "Smell the text." He had the same funny look on his face that you do.

I don't mean smell the pages of your Bible. I mean read with imagination. Sink yourself into the text. Stand there in the crowd, look over the shoulders of the disciples to hear what Jesus is saying. Walk next to Philip as he talks to the Ethiopian eunuch riding in his chariot. Float next to Moses in the reeds, lay in jail next to Jeremiah, and Peter, and Paul. Hear the Jordan River in the background of John the Baptist's preaching and the feet of the donkey crushing the palms as she carries Jesus down the Mount of Olives. Feel the mist of the cloud on your face when you go with Moses up Mount Sinai and with Jesus up the Mount of Transfiguration.

Smell the Sea of Galilee, the nets of the fishermen. Smell the lilies in the field where Jesus taught people not to worry. Smell Jerusalem, the sacrifices mixed with incense like a perpetual barbecue of mercy.

The smell gets you all the way there. You can see and hear from a distance, but to smell the thing, you have to be up close. Get up close to the Scriptures. Put your nose to work. Smell the breath of John the Baptist as he preaches repentance. Smell the fear of Abraham as he walks with Isaac to the altar of sacrifice. Smell the wood of David's lyre as he plays a psalm in his palace. Smell the despair as Job sits on the burning trash heap and scrapes his festering sores with a piece of broken pottery. Smell the sweet and looming danger as Eve grasps the forbidden fruit and pulls it off the branch, ripe and ready to devour. Smell the fresh hope in the garden when Jesus walks out of His grave in the still morning, alive again!

Reading with our nose helps fill in the details. It forces our imagination to recognize the reality of the text. It puts us up close, which is where the blessing is.

2. TALK BACK TO THE BOOK.

We often read passively, especially when we are reading out of duty. Our eyes march over the words while our minds are miles away. Instead, approach reading as a conversation with the author. This is true for any book, but an active reading is especially important as we engage the Scriptures. Mark the text. Circle important words, underline key verses, put question marks in the margin when something doesn't yet make sense. Talk back to the text. "Now, why would you say that, Paul?" "David, you are in a rage!" "Jesus, don't You see that they are in trouble?"

It is good for us to practice reading the Bible out loud. This is strange for many of us, but we want to engage the text with as much of our body as we can: our eyes and our ears, and our hands. This may mean giving preference to paper Bibles (as opposed to reading on a tablet or a phone). Holding a Bible in our hands, feeling the weight of the pages, opening and closing the book—all of these things help us engage personally with the text. (This, of course, is not a requirement but a suggestion. If you are in the habit of actively reading and engaging with the text on a screen, keep going!)

Reading the Bible as a back-and-forth exercise ropes our minds to the words.

3. LOOK FOR THE SURPRISE. KNOW THAT THERE IS SOMETHING NEW FOR YOU IN THE TEXT.

We think we know how the story ends. "I've read this before." "I know how things happen." Familiarity breeds contempt. Here is where the fight against "the Bible is a children's book" really happens. We remember these characters, we remember the plot, we think we've learned the text. But there is more, always more, in the Word of God.

It is one of the mysteries of the Scriptures that these eternal words are always new, and they make new. We open our Bibles expecting a surprise, and it always delivers something new and wonderful. God's Word is not sleepy, nor is it asleep. It awakens and enlightens.

> **The Word is so effective that whenever it is seriously contemplated, heard, and used, it is bound never to be without fruit. It always awakens new understanding, pleasure, and devoutness and produces a pure heart and pure thoughts. For these words are not lazy or dead, but are creative, living words.** (MARTIN LUTHER, LARGE CATECHISM, TEN COMMANDMENTS, 101)

We should expect these things when we crack open the Bible. We should expect that meditating on the text draws us into the adventure of theology and the surprise of God's redeeming story.

The Bible surprises us because God surprises us. He never acts like we expect Him to. In fact, we say with caution, He never acts like He ought to act. After all, He ought to destroy us, send us straight to eternal destruction. But He doesn't. He surprises us. Instead of giving us what we deserve, He rescues. He redeems. He is born, becomes sin for us, bears our sins, and carries our sorrows. He bleeds and dies. He breaks death's hold on us. He rises and ascends and gives us eternal life.

That is not predictable.

And all of it is for us.

This is the real surprise: the undeserved forgiveness of sins, the unexpected dawn of God's grace. His eternal mercy is new every morning, and the Lord intends to delight you with that newness every time you turn a page in your Bible.

4. READ THEOLOGICALLY.

St. Paul laments that the Corinthians still need baby food.

> But I, brothers, could not address you as spiritual people, but as people of the flesh, as infants in Christ. I fed you with milk, not solid food, for you were not ready for it. And even now you are not yet ready, for you are still of the flesh. (1 CORINTHIANS 3:1–3)

Most Christians contentedly drink milk their entire lives. They are never weaned. They never taste the solid food of doctrine. They never read the Bible theologically. They never get to the question of truth.

God's Word is true, and in it, we have access to otherwise hidden truths. The Scriptures unfold the mysteries of Christ, the mysteries of godliness, the wonderful and awesome things the Lord has done. Deep truths are found in the Scriptures. The most important of these—the truth of God, of man, of the beginning of everything and the end (or new beginning) of everything—are found *only* in the Scriptures.

These deep truths are called *theology*, a word that has, unfortunately, astonishingly, been made boring. That the devil has distracted and diverted our attention away from the wonder of God's Word must be one of his greatest accomplishments.

Imagine standing in one of the greatest and most fantastic cathedrals in Europe, and the guy next to you says, "Look at this," handing you a cartoon from the newspaper. In the same way, the devil does everything he can to divert our attention from the beauty and truth of the Scriptures to things trite, trivial, and stupid.

Reading the Bible theologically takes work. Instead of asking, "What does this mean to me?" a theological reading asks first, "What does this mean?" "What truth is the Holy Spirit teaching Christians with these words?" It means knowing the context, understanding the question that the text is answering. But above all, a theological reading of the Bible means knowing and rejoicing that the words of the Bible are true; they are Truth.

The Bible is a true account of history, a true account of humanity, a true account of God. Most of all, the Bible gives us the true height and depth of the love of Christ Jesus. His unknowable love is made known to us (see Ephesians 3:19).

Here is a mystery. A theological reading of the Bible does not uncover a different doctrine, but more, deeper, theology roots that reach down to the deep water. We don't move past the basics of the Bible, but further into them. We read the Bible as students eager to be taught.

> **I have more understanding than all my teachers, for
> Your testimonies are my meditation.** (Psalm 119:99)

What does this teach me about God? What does this teach me about myself? The world? How does this passage unveil the truth of the cosmos? The truth of truth? Of history? Of sin and repentance, of faith and forgiveness?

The Bible answers these questions. We read for the comfort and confidence of the answers.

5. DELIGHT IN GOD'S WORD.

One particularly frustrating afternoon, a fellow pastor challenged me: "Bryan, the Bible never says that we should read the Bible." I was sure he was wrong, and I tried to prove it. I couldn't. There is no command in the Bible that we should read the Bible.

We are commanded to meditate on the Bible, to treasure the Bible, to delight ourselves in God's Word.

It is not enough for us to read the Bible. We are to rejoice in it.

The blessed man's "delight is in the law of the LORD, and on His law he meditates day and night" (Psalm 1:2).

Delight. Let that word capture your imagination. What do you delight in? A cold drink on a hot day? A beautiful piece of art?

The Law of the Lord is "more to be desired . . . than gold, even much fine gold; sweeter also than honey and drippings of the honeycomb" (Psalm 19:10).

> **In the way of Your testimonies I delight as much as in all riches. I will meditate on Your precepts and fix my eyes on Your ways. I will delight in Your statutes; I will not forget Your word.** (PSALM 119:14–16)

THE

BIRD

IS THE

DEVIL

ST. PERPETUA: MARTYR. HERO.
AD 203. CARTHAGE.

Perpetua wrote the story of her own suffering when she was in jail. Second-century Christian author Tertullian preserved the account.

She was a young wife and mother, twenty-two years old, her only child still nursing. She came from a wealthy and noble family in Carthage. She believed in Jesus at a time when the Roman emperor forbade conversion to Christianity. She enrolled, with one of her brothers, as a catechumen even in a time of persecution.

She was arrested leaving church and thrown into a dungeon. Her father came to her, urging her to renounce her faith.

Perpetua pointed to a pitcher of water. "Do you see that pitcher?" "Yes" "Can you call it anything but a pitcher?" "No." "So can I call myself naught other than that which I am, a Christian."

In this first imprisonment, she had a dream of a thin bronze ladder that extended up into heaven. All along the ladder were instruments of death, and coiled around the bottom was a massive serpent. Perpetua stepped on the head of the serpent and then climbed up the ladder to a garden.

Perpetua's father came to her in prison, weeping and begging her to renounce her faith. "Have pity on us," he said. "Think of your mother and brother and sister." Perpetua said, "God's will be done."

Perpetua was brought to trial. The proconsul was named Hilarian. As she was in line, she heard the others before her

confessing Christ. As she stood before the judge, her father
came to her with her infant son in his arms. He said with
tears, "Perform the sacrifice! Have mercy on your child!"
Even Hilarian said, "Spare your father's gray hair. Spare the
infant. Make the sacrifice to Caesar." *Romans tolerant but must recognize Caesar as God*

Perpetua said, "I am a Christian."

Hilarian sentenced those who confessed to being Christian
to be killed by beasts. He sent them back to prison. "We
joyfully went," Perpetua wrote.

The night before they were to be given to the beasts
Perpetua had another dream. She was a gladiator fighting
with a great Egyptian. She triumphed over him, stomping his
head with her feet. When she awoke, she wrote, "I understood
that I should fight, not with beasts but against the devil; but
I knew that mine was the victory."

Perpetua was to be destroyed by a mad cow. She was
gorged. Her clothes were torn. "Stand fast in the faith," she
said to those suffering with her, "and love you all one another;
and be not offended because of our passion."

The impatient crowd demanded death for the Christians.
Perpetua and the others were lined up and, one by one, put
to death by the sword.

St. Perpetua: Martyr. Hero.

We'll meet in the resurrection.

young to shame the old

*father - pagan
mother - christian*

5

The Bird Is the Devil (Spiritual Warfare)

Do you?/ Submit to teaching of the Bible or go their own way

*When anyone hears the word of the kingdom
and does not understand it, the evil one comes
and snatches away what has been sown in his heart.
This is what was sown along the path.*

(MATTHEW 13:19)

no roots / ground packed

The bird in Jesus' parable is the devil.

The devil snatches away.

He attacks God's kingdom. He attacks God's Word. He attacks everything that the Lord is and does.

He is not content as long as there is any light and any life in the world. He prowls around like a roaring lion, seeking someone to devour. He lurks like a ravenous wolf dressed in sheepskin. The devil comes to the earth in a rage, knowing that his time is short. He flutters like a bird ready to snatch up the seed as it is sown.

He is restless and furious.

He is your enemy. You are under attack.

We simply can't read the Bible without bumping into the uncomfortable fact that we are at war, that we have enemies who want to see us

41

destroyed. We must give up the idea that the Christian life is a peaceful or quiet life. It wasn't true for Jesus, and it isn't true for Christians. The kingdom of God is assaulted, assailed, and attacked. You, dear Christian, are in that kingdom. The mighty fortress of God, the city of the Lord, is surrounded, besieged, and bombarded.

The more we understand the Scriptures, the more we know that our lives are embattled. Our Baptism drafts us into a military service, and we are, as Paul says to Timothy, "a good soldier of Christ Jesus" (2 Timothy 2:3), set in this world to fight the good fight of faith.

The devil attacks us, and we are set in this world to stand against him, to resist him. Informed by God's Word, we are not ignorant of his tactics.

This section is like a military briefing for soldiers in the spiritual battle. We'll search the Scriptures to see what we can know about this spiritual battle: how the devil fights, how Jesus fights, and how we survive. We'll answer seven questions about spiritual warfare so that, in the end, we might "be able to stand against the schemes of the devil" (Ephesians 6:11).

1. Where did this warfare start?

2. Who is at war, and what is the war about?

3. Who is on our side?

4. Where is the fight taking place?

5. What are the weapons and the tactics of the enemy?

6. What is our gear? How do we fight?

7. What is victory?

6

A Declaration of War

I will put enmity between you and the woman,
and between your offspring and her offspring;
He shall bruise your head,
and you shall bruise His heel.

(GENESIS 3:15)

Where did this war start?

Would you be surprised to know that it was in the beginning, in the Garden of Eden? I imagine you could guess that. But perhaps it comes as a surprise that it was started by God.

Here's how it happened.

God planted a garden for Adam and Eve. There they were to live out their "very-goodness" in the Lord's name, bringing forth life in their own family and blessing all of creation with their rule and dominion. They were given perfect fellowship with God, with each other, and with all of creation. There was life, an abundance of life and joy.

Adam and Eve were to serve each other with love and to worship God with faith. This is why the Lord planted the tree of the knowledge of good and evil in the garden. This tree was their chapel where they could worship God by faith, believing what they could not see (and were never supposed to see): death.

Adam and Eve were to confess this creed: "I believe that on the day that we would eat of this tree, we would surely die" (see Genesis 2:17).

It's amazing to think of the contrast. We, on this side of the fall, see nothing but death all around us. So we worship by faith and confess what we don't see: "I believe in the resurrection of the body and the life everlasting." We see sin all around us, but we worship by faith and confess what we cannot see: "I believe in the forgiveness of sins." But Adam and Eve are surrounded by life and perfection. For them to believe and confess what they cannot see, they worship by faith, confessing, "When we eat, we die."

The devil, though, visited this first church and preached a different doctrine. He questioned God's Word: "Did God really say . . . ?" He gave them an alternative promise, "You will not surely die." He made God the enemy: "God knows what will really happen when you eat." Eve listened and believed the devil. Eve and then Adam took the fruit and ate. They disbelieved God. They disobeyed God. And on that day, they died.

This was a double death—a spiritual and a physical death. The spiritual death came immediately. The physical death would follow.

As a result of their disobedience, they now saw their nakedness as shameful, and they took it upon themselves to cover their shame with fig leaves. We note in passing that all the sons and daughters of Adam and Eve are continually trying to find new fig leaves—new works and new religions with which we can hide ourselves from God or cover the shame of our sins. We also note that Adam and Eve seemed particularly pleased with their new dress—that is, until they hear the sound of the Lord walking in the garden.

Those footsteps were terrifying.

With horror, Adam and Eve realize that their fig leaves are not enough. They run and hide in the bushes, holding their breath, hoping the Lord won't find them and destroy them.

We'll pause and let the situation sink in.

Adam and Eve had fallen. They had brought death into the world. They were now at war with each other, at war with creation, at war with God. The only peaceful relationship in the garden was between Adam and Eve and the devil. It is shocking to consider that Adam and Eve were running *from* God and *with* the devil. They were hiding from God and with the devil. There was peace with the devil.

God does find them. He does not destroy them. In fact, and you must see this with your imagination, the Lord finds Adam and Eve hiding with the serpent, and He questions them in turn: Adam first, then Eve, then the devil. And it is as a result of God's questions that we get the declaration of war.

The Lord says to the devil,

> **I will put enmity between you and the woman,**
>   **and between your offspring[1] and her offspring;**
> **He shall bruise your head,**
>   **and you shall bruise His heel."** (GENESIS 3:15)

This text is a riddle and a beautiful, life-giving promise. The Church has called it the *protoevangelium*, "the first Good News." It is the promise that Eve would have a Son who would have the divine power and authority to destroy the devil, and in that destruction, He would also be destroyed. Stunning!

God finds Adam and Eve at peace with the devil and says, "No. I will put enmity between you. There will be war between the devil and humanity." Likewise, God finds Himself at war with us, and He says, "No. I won't have it. I will not be at war with you. There will be peace between heaven and earth, peace between God and man." It reminds us of St. Paul: "Therefore, since we have been justified by faith, we have peace with God through our Lord Jesus Christ" (Romans 5:1).

God declares peace between us and Himself, and in so doing, He sets us at war with the devil.

Spiritual death / physical death (handwritten)

Get along & don't / easy / leaves you alone / world gets along (handwritten)

---

1   Some English translations prefer the more archaic word *seed.*

7

The Liar and the Lie

For this reason God will send them strong delusion,
that they should believe the lie.

(2 THESSALONIANS 2:11 NKJV)

[The devil] was a murderer from the beginning,
and does not stand in the truth, because there is no
truth in him. When he lies, he speaks out of his own
character, for he is a liar and the father of lies.

(JOHN 8:44)

The devil is a liar.

He comes to "steal and kill and destroy" (John 10:10), and the way he steals, murders, and wrecks is through lies. He lied in the beginning. He lies to the end. He lies in every which way to deceive us, confuse us, confound us, and throw us off of the truth of God's Word and the comfort of His Gospel.

Martin Luther calls the devil the "master of a thousand arts" (Large Catechism, Preface, 12). The devil tempts, he troubles, he preaches, he deceives, he confounds, he wounds, he attacks, he leaves in peace, he possesses, he destroys, he sows discontent and disorder, he quotes the Bible, he offers the world, he befriends, he beguiles, he betrays, and he acts in all these ways contrary to God. But when you boil it all down, you come to this: the devil lies.

He lies about himself. He lies about you. He lies about your neighbor. He lies about God. He lies about God's Word, the Law and the Gospel. He lies about the past, the future, the good and the bad. He lies about everything. He is a liar.

Jesus says of the devil that "there is no truth in him. When he lies, he speaks out of his own character, for he is a liar and the father of lies" (John 8:44). Lies, lies, everywhere lies.

In an amazing and challenging passage, though, St. Paul speaks not about "lies" but about "the lie," one lie:

> **For this reason God will send them strong delusion, that they should believe the lie.** (2 Thessalonians 2:11 NKJV)

What is "the lie"? Paul could have said "that they should believe all the different sorts and kinds of lies that the devil speaks." He doesn't. He speaks of the singular, the one lie.

This is difficult. How can we understand all the different ways that the devil lies and deceives as a singular lie? What is the essence of his lie?

I'd like to suggest an approach to this question.

On the one hand, the devil loves to work in darkness and confusion. He loves the mist. He hates it when we can name a thing, identify a thing, and understand what a thing is. He never wants us to see clearly what he is doing. He lives in deception.

On the other hand, the devil cannot create. He can only destroy. He can only strike at the things that God has put in place.

This means that we can identify the devil's works not by looking at his works but by looking at the works of God that he attacks. This is a general principle when it comes to understanding the devil's work.

For example, we see divorce, we see people tempted to sexual confusion, we see immorality, we see court cases reworking the legal definition of marriage, we see husbands and wives growing apart, and it is confounding. But all of it is the devil's assault on the Lord's institution of marriage. The devil is anti-marriage.

Another example: we see hundreds of different churches with all sorts of different doctrines. Some insist that by good works we can earn our way into heaven; some make Baptism our work; some preach that true faith is manifest in charismatic gifts. It seems as if there is a new flavor of false doctrine announced every day, and it is confounding. But all of it is the devil's assault on the preaching of the Gospel. The devil is anti-Gospel, anti-Christ.

There is a unity, not in the devil's attacks, but in the things of God that he attacks.

We can identify "the lie" of the devil when we know what "the truth" is. The truth of the Scripture is this:

Jesus is Lord.

Or, to say the exact same thing with slightly different words:

Jesus is the Savior.

This is the simple teaching of the Bible, the simple preaching of the Gospel. It is the essential creed of the Christian faith. "The lie" is anything and everything that assaults or stands against this truth.

The lie is this: Jesus is *not* the Savior.

We can imagine, then, all the different forms this lie can take.

"You don't need saving." That's one way to do it. "You're a good person. You don't need help." "You are so good that God will be happy to have you in heaven."

"Jesus is *a* savior." That's another form of the lie that seems to work. "Jesus might be your truth, but not my truth; certainly not *the* truth." "There are lots of other saviors. Every road leads to heaven. All religions are the same."

"You are the savior." You save yourself. Your works, your decision, your whatever is the reason you are saved.

"Jesus is their Savior, but not yours." You are too sinful, too wicked, too wounded, whatever. This is another form of the lie.

"If you believe that Jesus is the Savior, then people will think you are a fool."

"If Jesus is the Savior, then things should be better."

The devil distorts the truth in a thousand different ways. He mutilates the Lord's truth. He lies. And he lies with the purpose of convincing you that the truth is not true, that Jesus is not the Savior.

This is the war, the spiritual battle we are in.

By the devil's lie, we fall and die.

In the Lord's truth, we stand and we live.

8

The Field of Battle: The Three Estates and the Castle of the Conscience

*Woe to you, O earth and sea, for the
devil has come down to you in great wrath,
because he knows that his time is short!*
(Revelation 12:12)

Where does the spiritual battle take place? Where is the battlefield?

This is a tricky question, because it is not a physical location. We don't want to say that the spiritual battle is more intense in Colorado than it is in Texas or that the battle is raging in France but not in Uganda. (I do think we can identify unique demonic strategies at work in different cultures. For example, secularism rages in the West while Islamism has filled the Middle East. There is a prevalence of spiritism in Africa and mysticism in the East.) The location of spiritual warfare will not be physically identifiable.

There are two unique ways to approach this question.

First, we see that the devil fights against the three estates instituted by God. Second, we see that the devil fights against the Word in the source, the means, and the goal. We'll consider these in turn.

THE THREE ESTATES

First, the three estates. We see from the Scriptures that the Lord has ordered this world with three realms: the church, the family, and the state. We identify these as the three estates. The church and the family were instituted by God in the Garden of Eden. The state was instituted after the fall.

The church was instituted by God for the preaching of the Word, and after the fall, the church chiefly exists to forgive sins and give the Lord's gift of eternal life.

The family was instituted by God when He united Adam and Eve in holy matrimony, gave them dominion over the earth, and blessed them with the instructions to "be fruitful and multiply" (Genesis 1:28). The family exists to bring forth and support earthly life.

The state was instituted after the fall into sin. God instituted the sword to punish and curb sin, and those who bear the sword are the state. The state exists to limit sin through punishment and coercion. We see that the sword can be pointed externally (waging just war) and internally (police, judges, jails, etc.). The state guards and protects; it brings forth little deaths to prevent greater deaths.

Part of the genius of the Lutheran Reformation was the insight that all of us live in all three estates. Prior to the Reformation, the estates were understood to be exclusive. You were either part of those who pray (the priests, monks, and nuns; holy orders), those who fight (the royalty and soldiers), or those who work (the peasants, farmers, merchants, regular families, etc.). In fact, the vow to become a monk was essentially a vow to not be part of the family (celibacy), the working class (poverty), or the ruling class (obedience to the order).

When Martin Luther, then a monk, saw clearly from the Scriptures that salvation was by faith, this entire system of separate estates came tumbling down. If Jesus' righteousness belongs to the Christian by faith, then no life or estate is holier than any other. The father and the mother are just as holy as the monk and nun. The farmer and the soldier are just as holy as the priest and the pope.

As the medieval structure of the three estates crumbled, Luther could see the foundation underneath, and it was wonderful to see. The Lord has instituted these three realms for all of us—the church, the family, and the state.

Further, Luther recognized that these three estates acted as walls to protect the conscience. Imagine a castle designed with three concentric walls, one within the other. To get to the heart, the enemy would have to destroy each of these walls. These walls are the state, the home, and the church.

Luther talks about it in his 1539 *On the Councils and the Church*. This is a longer quotation, but it's worth our attention.

> But God must be over all and nearest to all, *to preserve this ring or circle against the devil*, and to do everything in all of life's vocations, indeed, in all creatures. Thus Psalm 127 [:1] says that there are only two temporal governments on earth, that of *the city* and that of *the home*, "Unless the Lord builds the house; unless the Lord watches over the city." The first government is that of the home, from which the people come; the second is that of the city, meaning the country, the people, princes and lords, which we call the secular government. These embrace everything—children, property, money, animals, etc. The home must produce, whereas the city must guard, protect, and defend. Then follows the third, God's own home and city, that is, *the church*, which must obtain people from the home and protection and defense from the city. These are the three hierarchies ordained by God, and we need no more; indeed, we have enough and more than enough to do in living aright and resisting the devil in these three. (AE 41:176–77, EMPHASIS ADDED)

The devil is always attacking the three estates. He attacks the church with false doctrine and unholy living. He attacks the home with strife and confusion. He attacks the state with all sorts of trouble and difficulties. Knowing this helps us understand what is going on in the world. This is why there are Supreme Court cases to define marriage and why neighbors have so many fights. These are assaults on the estate of the family. It helps us understand why congregations are in conflict, why there are false doctrines, sects, and divisions. The devil attacks the estate of the church. This is why there are wars, unrest, and constant political battles. The devil works to undermine the state.

There is a spiritual battle in every home, in every church, and in every state house. And there is a broader war on the general condition of these three estates. In other words, the devil attacks every family, but he also attacks the idea of family. He attacks every church where the Word of God is preached, but he also attacks the very idea of religion. The devil attacks every nation, but he also attacks the idea of nations and the various political doctrines.

Yet the destruction of the church, the family, and the state is not his ultimate goal. He is after people. Everything he does is to get to the conscience. The devil besieges the rings and walls of protection to get access to the hearts and minds of the Lord's people. A spiritual battle happens in the culture, but this is only the first wave of the attack; the second wave takes place in the heart, the place where the Lord intends for His Word to find a home.

THE CASTLE OF THE CONSCIENCE
AND THE ATTACK OF THE WORD ON THE WAY

And this brings us to the second way of addressing the question regarding the battlefield of spiritual warfare. If the devil is attacking the Word of God, he will attack the source, the means, and the goal of the Word.

In the parable of the sower, the birds will go after the seed while it is in the sower's satchel, in the air, and when it lands on the ground. This means that the three points of attack are (1) the heavenly council, that is, the throne room of God; (2) the church where the Word is preached; and (3) the heart where the Word is received by faith.

First, the heavenly council. The Lord sits enthroned. The Bible gives us, now and then, glimpses into this heavenly court. Isaiah saw it as he was serving in the temple (Isaiah 6). John is brought there as a visitor in the Revelation of Jesus given to him. Jeremiah notes that the mark of the true prophet is that he has stood in the council of the Lord (see Jeremiah 23:18, 22).

In that heavenly court, there is a conversation between the Father, the Son, and the Holy Spirit. (That conversation and council is what the prophets are to make known on earth.) In that place, requests are made and petitions are heard. (These are the prayer of the Church.) There is worship there, the angels and saints falling down before the Lord and singing His praises. That throne room is also a courtroom. That is what is most important for this conversation.

Recall the first part of Job. There was an assembly of the holy angels, and Satan also comes before the throne of God. "Satan" means accuser, a prosecuting attorney, and that is exactly what he does. The Lord extols His servant Job, and the devil says, "Job only believes because You've made his life so easy." We'll consider the drama that unfolds in future chapters. Now, it is enough for us to notice that the devil attacks the Word at the source, in the throne room of heaven.

This, in fact, is a frightful thing to realize: the devil accuses us before God in heaven. He attacks the heavenly verdict that we are righteous and holy. But there is comfort for us as well. Revelation 12 especially delivers this comfort.

John sees the vision of a pregnant woman. This is Old Testament Israel, waiting for the promise of Genesis 3:15 to be fulfilled. This woman is pregnant with the Messiah. There is a dragon waiting to devour the Baby when He is born. The Child is born; the dragon fails. The Child is caught up to God and to His throne (Revelation 12:5). In this one phrase we have contained not only the birth but also the ministry, life, teaching, crucifixion, death, burial, resurrection, and ascension of Jesus.

What happens next is fascinating and wonderful. Jesus brings His victory, His blood, His triumph over sin, death, and the devil with Him into the heavenly throne room, and there no longer is any place for the devil. There is nothing for him to do, no accusation to bring against sinners that has not been answered by the atoning sacrifice of Christ on the cross.

Imagine it like this. You are on trial before God. Satan is the accuser, and he brings your sin before the court. As soon as he tries to admit the evidence of your guilt, Jesus, your Advocate, your Defender, stands up and says, "Objection: that sin is forgiven."

Every time the devil tries to bring an accusation against you, Jesus is there at your side. "Objection: that sin is died for. Objection: I suffered for that sin already. Objection: My blood covers that sin. Objection: I carried that sin away." The death of Jesus stands as the evidence for your righteousness. The blood of Jesus is the chief witness in your case. Because of this, there is "now no condemnation for those who are in Christ Jesus" (Romans 8:1).

When Jesus, the Lamb who was slain, who is raised, who is ascended, takes His place at the right hand of the Father, then a war breaks out in heaven, and the victory of the crucifixion and resurrection are brought to bear on the devil. Here's the account in all of its glory:

> Now war arose in heaven, Michael and his angels fighting against the dragon. And the dragon and his angels fought back, but he was defeated, and there was no longer any place for them in heaven. And the great dragon was thrown down, that ancient serpent, who is called the devil and Satan, the deceiver of the whole world—he was thrown down to the earth, and his angels were thrown down with him. And I heard a loud voice in heaven, saying, "Now the salvation and the power and the kingdom of our God and the authority of His Christ have come, for the accuser of our brothers has been thrown down, who accuses them day and night before our God. And they have conquered him by the blood of the Lamb and by the word

of their testimony, for they loved not their lives even unto
death. Therefore, rejoice, O heavens and you who dwell
in them! (REVELATION 12:7–12)

What a vision! What a triumph! The accuser, the ancient serpent,
has been cast out of heaven. The devil would love to attack the Word
of God at the source, where it comes out of the very mouth of God, but
he can't. Not, at least, for the Christian. The devil has been removed
from that place. He no longer accuses you before the Father's throne.
Where, then, can the devil attack the preaching of the Word?

But woe to you, O earth and sea, for the devil has come
down to you in great wrath, because he knows that his time
is short! (REVELATION 12:12B)

The devil doesn't want God's Word to get to you. He doesn't want it
to be pure when it does reach your ears. He wants to snatch the Word
of God right out of the air on its way to the ground of your heart. He
attacks the church, the pastors and teachers, and he attacks the doctrine;
he attacks the hearer and the hearing of the Word. He makes it hard
for you to go to church. He makes it hard for the church to continue.

Have you ever wondered why Sunday mornings are so difficult?
Why waking up and driving to church seems much more difficult than
it ought to? Why listening to a sermon is such hard work? Or have you
wondered about why things are so difficult in the church, why there
never seems to be peace, but there is always trouble? The Word of God
is always opposed, and getting our ears and our hearts to the place where
they hear God's Word is spiritual warfare.

Here's why.

The preaching and teaching of God's Word is the supply line for the
Christian life.

Consider a war. When two nations are at war, the "front" is where
the soldiers are on the front lines of battle. Supply lines are used to
deliver to these soldiers the things they need—ammunition, medical
supplies, food, and so on. One particularly effective tactic is to attack

the supply lines. If you can cut off the supply of food and weapons, then the soldiers are helpless.

The Word of God is the supply line for the Church Militant.

All of our spiritual blessings and benefits are delivered to us through the Word.

Martin Luther makes a very helpful distinction between the "winning" of forgiveness and the "delivery" of forgiveness. The forgiveness of sins is won for us by the death of Jesus on the cross. Forgiveness is delivered in the Word. Here's how Luther says it:

> So that our readers may the better perceive our teaching I shall clearly and broadly describe it. We treat of the forgiveness of sins in two ways. First, how it is achieved and won. Second, how it is distributed and given to us. Christ has achieved it on the cross, it is true. But he has not distributed or given it on the cross. He has not won it in the supper or sacrament. There he has distributed and given it through the Word, as also in the gospel, where it is preached. He has won it once for all on the cross. But the distribution takes place continuously, before and after, from the beginning to the end of the world. For inasmuch as he had determined once to achieve it, it made no difference to him whether he distributed it before or after, through his Word, as can easily be proved from Scripture. But now there is neither need nor time to do so.

> If now I seek the forgiveness of sins, I do not run to the cross, for I will not find it given there. Nor must I hold to the suffering of Christ, as Dr. Karlstadt trifles, in knowledge or remembrance, for I will not find it there either. But I will find in the sacrament or gospel the word which distributes, presents, offers, and gives to me that forgiveness which was won on the cross. Therefore, Luther has rightly taught that whoever has a bad conscience from his sins should go to the sacrament and obtain comfort, not

> because of the bread and wine, not because of the body
> and blood of Christ, but because of the word which in the
> sacrament offers, presents, and gives the body and blood
> of Christ, given and shed for me. Is that not clear enough?
>
> (AE 40:213–14)

While it's funny that Luther refers to himself in the third person, it is of the utmost importance that we know how the Lord Jesus gets His mercy and forgiveness to us in the preaching of the Word. The Word of God brings the promise of mercy and God's kindness to us here and now. The Word of God transports the victory of Jesus on the cross through space and time and carries it right into our conscience.

It is no wonder, then, that the devil attacks the Word, the preaching, the Church.

It is very difficult to imagine the survival of saving faith apart from the regular hearing of God's Word. Hebrews reminds us of this:

> **Let us hold fast the confession of our hope without
> wavering, for He who promised is faithful. And let us con-
> sider how to stir up one another to love and good works,
> not neglecting to meet together, as is the habit of some,
> but encouraging one another, and all the more as you see
> the Day drawing near.** (HEBREWS 10:23–25)

This important text reminds us that the gathering together of Christians will be more and more important the closer we are to the end. In other words, going to church is more important now than it ever was, and every year it will be more and more important. Christians support one another, bless one another, strengthen one another with the Lord's Word.

The picture the old preachers used to teach this is helpful. Imagine trying to start a campfire with only one log. It's almost impossible. For a fire to burn, you need many logs stacked up together. And when the fire is going, if you take one log out, it will eventually cool off and burn out. So it is with Christians. We are not supposed to go at this alone.

Our faith is designed to work in groups. Our faith lives by the preaching of the Word and the receiving of the Lord's body and blood.

We need, in a truly desperate sense, God's Word to be delivered to us. The Word is the supply chain. It is the armory. The church is the supply drop. It is the field hospital.

We might be tempted to think that spiritual warfare happens outside the church (and true enough, the devil walks to and fro on the earth), but the most intense spiritual battles happen around the preaching of God's Word. The church is the field of battle, and this means, at the very least, we go to church.

The devil opposes the delivery of the Word. We fight back when we hear and delight and believe the Word and promises of God.

Third, the devil fights in our conscience. He comes to tempt and confuse. He comes lying and deceiving. He tries to steal away God's life-giving Word and replace it with the tares of false doctrine and empty spirituality.

The devil wages war in the Christian's heart, and his hope is that we would have a bad conscience. A conscience can be bad in many different ways, and it can be bad in different ways at the same time:

> A prideful conscience thinks that it has kept the Law and has obtained a righteousness on its own.

> A hardened or calloused conscience thinks that the Law doesn't apply to it, that we are each a law unto ourselves.

> A despairing conscience thinks that the Gospel doesn't apply to it, that "I am too miserable a sinner to be forgiven or loved by God."

> An indifferent conscience doesn't care about spiritual things at all; it is asleep, ignorant of the most important things, the preaching of Law and Gospel.

All of these are distorted consciences, consciences shaped by the devil's lies.

These are the devil's aims and goals in the spiritual fight. We will consider how the devil attacks in the next chapters. It is enough for us to consider here that the devil brings the spiritual fight right to us, to our minds, to our hearts, and to our consciences. We want to know that his aim is to destroy our consciences, and we want to rejoice that the Lord's aim is the opposite.

The aim of our charge is love that issues from a pure heart and a good conscience and a sincere faith. (1 TIMOTHY 1:5)

Jesus gives us a good conscience, a working conscience, and a clean and comforted conscience. The Law shows us what righteousness and love look like and how we should live. The Law shows us that we are sinners in desperate need of salvation. The Gospel forgives our sins through the death and resurrection of Jesus. The Holy Spirit teaches and moves us to love and bless our neighbors. This is a how the Lord gives us a good conscience, a repentant conscience.

In the end, Jesus stands on the battlefield of the conscience. He triumphs over sin, death, and the devil. He forgives our sins. The victory shout of Jesus echoes in the good conscience: "It is finished!"

9

The Devil's Tactic: Attack Repentance

We are not ignorant of [Satan's] designs.

(2 Corinthians 2:11)

The Bible exposes the devils tactics and strategies.

The devil might be the "master of a thousand arts," tempting us and coming at us from every direction, but, simply put, he has but one aim: to kill eternally. He has one weapon: lies.

To state his work clearly: the devil attacks repentance.

The best way, then, to understand the devil's strategy is to understand repentance.

First, repentance is God's work in us. "Restore us, O Lord, and cause Your face to shine," David prays in Psalm 80 (see vv. 3, 7, and 19). We read in the Book of Acts how God gives and grants repentance (see 5:31 and 11:18).

Second, repentance consists of two parts: contrition and faith.

Repentance is the right reception of the truth of God: Jesus is the Savior. In that simple preaching, we learn that we need a Savior (the Law) and that we have a Savior (the Gospel).

Contrition is knowing that we need a Savior. It is sorrow over our sins. Contrition is what happens when God the Holy Spirit holds up the mirror of His Law to show us our sins. Contrition is a godly sorrow, a knowledge that we have broken God's Law, and more, that because of our sins and failures, we have deserved God's wrath and anger.

Faith, on the other hand, is a trust in God's promise, and specifically a trust in the promise that the death of Jesus forgives us all our sins. Faith trusts in the mercy and kindness of God; it relies on the death and resurrection of Jesus. Faith knows that Jesus, in His death, stood between me and God's wrath, that He was my substitute on the cross, and that the wrath and anger of God that I deserve has been spent on Christ. Faith, then, is joyful and confident to live and to die because it knows that there is no condemnation for those who are in Christ Jesus.

Good works are the fruit of repentance. The Christian's love for God and for neighbor grow out of repentance.

Repentance, then, is nothing other than the appropriate reception of God's Word of Law and Gospel. The Law comes and preaches to us, showing us our sin, our failure, our desperate wickedness, our lack of love, and whatever else is filthy and rebellious in us, and we are contrite. The Gospel comes with the sweet and glorious Good News that the Son of God came in our flesh and blood to bear our sins and be our Redeemer and Savior, and we believe it. The Law works contrition. The Gospel works faith. (And then both play their parts in the resulting love expressed in the Christian life.)

Third, repentance is not a one-time event. It is not the emotional experience at the end of the revival service when, prompted by some self-styled evangelist, I surrender my life to Jesus. No, repentance is a constant reality for the Christian. Jesus tells us to take up our cross *daily* and follow Him. Luther reminds us that our Baptism sets us up to fight our flesh through daily contrition and repentance. The Christian life is a life of repentance.

If we live by repentance, we die by unrepentance. The devil's aim is this death: to attack and destroy the life of repentance in the Christian heart.

He attacks the preaching of the Law and our contrition, and he attacks the preaching of the Gospel and our faith. We'll consider both in turn.

THE DEVIL'S ATTACK ON THE PREACHING OF THE LAW

First, the attack on the Law and contrition. This attack is at least twofold.

The devil doesn't want us to hear the Law at all. He wants us to be led by our sinful flesh, to be driven this way and that by our sinful desires. The Holy Spirit preaches the Law to tell us what we ought to do. The devil preaches in such a way that we think we need no law at all, that we are a law unto ourselves, that we can live however we want. The devil loves this kind of lawlessness.

He does this trick. The devil knows that we have a sinful flesh and that our flesh has sinful wants and desires. (The old theologians called this *concupiscence*, the inborn inclination toward sin.) The devil knows that we are rebellious, angry, lustful, greedy, lazy, deceitful, and discontented. We want to sin. (See, for example, Galatians 5:16–21.) The devil, then, comes alongside our sinful flesh and says, "Hey, you want to sin, do you?"

"Yes," our flesh says.

"Well, I've got good news," the devil says. "I want you to sin too!"

"Okay," our flesh answers back.

"I want you to be free to do what you want to do. Don't you want that freedom?" the devil lies.

"Yes, I would love that freedom," our flesh says, driven by a love of itself and its sin.

"Well, God doesn't want you to have that freedom. He wants you to be His slave, to live like He wants you to live. That's why He gave the Law, to put you in bondage. The only thing between you and this freedom that you want (and that I want for you) is God's Law. Throw it off. Break its bonds. Live how I, er, *you* want to live." The devil bows, resting his case, having told our sinful flesh just what it wants to hear.

Time after time I've seen this argument work. There is a particular sin that people fall in love with, normally a sexual sin. They know that it is wrong, that it is against God's Law. If they would think about it for a minute, they would also see that it is foolish. But the flesh and the desires of the flesh are strong, and the devil comes along with lies that support the flesh. He preaches sermons to justify sin. His sermons rally the flesh to throw off all constraints.

I wonder sometimes how many people leave the faith and become atheists simply because they wanted to move in with their boyfriend or girlfriend.

This is the first attack on contrition: to snatch up the preaching of the Law so that it doesn't reach the conscience, to mute the preaching of God's right and wrong. Often, to make this work, the devil will provide an alternative law, an alternative morality, a different standard by which I can feel good about myself.

Next is the second attack on contrition: the Holy Spirit preaches the Law to show me that I am a sinner; the devil preaches a law to convince me that I am a good person.

He might use God's Law to do it, or he might help us invent a law of our own. I'm convinced this accounts for all the alternative moralities constantly taking shape around us. The morality of tolerance, the morality of environmentalism, the morality of the sexual revolution—all these have a new definition of good and evil. We see the devil's game. These alternative moralities let me sin in the way that I want to sin, and I can still consider myself a good person. I might be sexually immoral, but I am helping the environment. I might be rebellious and angry, but at least I don't condemn other people's ideas.

Beware the alternate moralities. They are part of the devil's attack on true contrition.

The devil can even work this trick with God's Law. The Pharisees are the prime example of this tactic. They had Moses and the Ten Commandments, but instead of seeing their own sin, they were proud. The devil had used the Law to preach a righteousness of their own, a righteousness of the Law. They were the Law keepers. They were the ones who could stand on their own two feet on Judgment Day, equipped with an impressive résumé of works and efforts that would commend themselves. They are the ones who do not need a Savior; they have managed to save themselves. There is no contrition here, no sorrow over sin.

The devil works this angle in the Christian heart, exalting our own works, our own efforts, our own goodness in our imagination so that we, too, become proud. The Law no longer shows us our sin. The mirror has become so dim that we see our reflection and are impressed by it. Pride replaces contrition, and we no longer need a Savior. There is no contrition because there is no sin, no failing, nothing to be sorry about.

These are, at least in summary, the two ways the devil attacks the Law and contrition.

THE DEVIL'S ATTACK ON THE PREACHING OF THE GOSPEL

He also attacks the preaching of the Gospel. He tempts us to unbelief, false belief, and despair.

The devil hates the Good News that Jesus has died on the cross for sinners. He hates the Gospel promise that our sins are forgiven by Jesus and that we are justified by faith in His mercy apart from our own works and efforts. The devil wants us to go back to the Garden of Eden, back to that time when we were content with our fig leaves, when we were hiding with him in the trees. That was when God was angry with us. That was before the Gospel had been spoken and believed.

The devil remembers how he got us there. He questioned God's Word. He said, "Did God really say?" He preaches that same sermon, and he brings that question, that doubt, straight to God's Gospel promises.

Remember the Baptism and temptation of Jesus (Matthew 3:13–4:11). When Jesus came up out of the water of the Jordan River, a voice from heaven said, "This is My beloved Son, in whom I am well pleased" (Matthew 3:17). This promise is spoken to Jesus from heaven. (This is one of only three times that we hear the voice of God the Father in the Gospels!) Then, when He is driven by the Holy Spirit into the wilderness to be tempted by the devil, it is this promise, spoken in Baptism, that the devil attacks. "If You are the Son of God, command these stones to become loaves of bread" (Matthew 4:3). If? "You are My beloved Son" is what the voice said. There is nothing more certain than this. There are no ifs involved. Jesus is God's Son. But the devil attacks this certainty. He attacks this promise. And he keeps attacking it.

"If You are the Son of God, throw Yourself down" (Matthew 4:6). The devil attacks the promise of Baptism. He did it with Jesus, and he does it with us.

When we were baptized, the Lord adopted us into His family (see Galatians 3:25–27). He gave us His name, the name of the Father and of the Son and of the Holy Spirit (Matthew 28:19). He forgave us all our sins (Acts 2:38; 22:16). Jesus gives the glorious promise that "whoever believes and is baptized will be saved" (Mark 16:16).

These promises belong to us, the Lord's people, the baptized. The devil comes along putting ifs and buts before these promises.

First, the devil tempts us to unbelief. "You trust the Bible? That's just a bunch of fairy tales! You think that the death of a man in Palestine two thousand years ago can help you today? Science has proven that the Bible is false, and you are putting your faith in it? If there really was a God, don't you think things would be better? Don't you think God would show Himself to you?"

Second, he tempts us to false belief or confused doctrine. The devil especially tries to mix together the Law and the Gospel. Salvation is one part God, one part me. "Jesus died for you, but what have you done for Him? You haven't done enough to be saved. God did His part, and now it's up to you."

The Judaizers were the best at this tactic. They followed Paul around as he started churches, and as soon as he left town, they would set up shop. "Paul said that you are justified by God's grace through faith, but that's not enough. You must be circumcised. You must observe the Sabbath. You must keep the Law of Moses. Faith in the Gospel is not enough." The devil has his Judaizers today, preachers who add in the necessity of our works for salvation. This is another assault of the devil on the preaching of the Gospel.

Third, he tempts us to despair of God's mercy. "How could God love you? Look at what you've done! You call yourself a Christian?" He tempts

CHAPTER 9 | THE DEVIL'S TACTIC: ATTACK REPENTANCE

us to think that we've outsinned the Lord's mercy, that we are too bad, too dirty, too unclean to belong to God.

I remember talking once with a person who was convinced that God couldn't forgive him, that he had committed "too many sins." "That is amazing," I responded. "I've never met anyone that good at sinning, someone whose sins are so strong that Jesus can't forgive them. You must be greater than Jesus Himself!"

"Well, no," he responded.

"I didn't think so." Jesus is a better Savior than you are a sinner. Your sins cannot undo His cross. You cannot manage a stain that the blood of Jesus cannot wash. Christ Jesus came to save sinners. Jesus is not the Savior of little sinners, baby sinners. Jesus is the Savior of David and Moses, of Peter and Paul, of you and me. He has taken the enemies of God and redeemed them, redeemed us.

The devil wants us to despair of God's mercy. He wants us to think that the cross is not for us, that the love of God does not reach us, that the promises of God do not apply to us. This is the lie. The cross and the blood of Jesus are for you.

> **Behold the Lamb of God, who takes away the sin of the world.** (JOHN 1:29)

This preaching from the Jordan River still stands. It stands true for you.

And, ironically, delightfully, one of the ways we know it stands is because the devil attacks it so furiously. When we see the devil in a rage trying to undo the great promises of the Gospel, we know we are on to something wonderful and true.

All of this adds up to the same thing, the same anti-sermon: the devil tempts us to think that all the good things God promised you in your Baptism were lies.

Tertullian, a Father of the Church, keenly observed this demonic tactic.

> **Happy is our sacrament of water, in that, by washing away the sins of our early blindness, we are set free and admitted into eternal life! . . . But we, little fishes, after the example of our [Fish] ΙΧΘΥΣ Jesus Christ, are born**

in water, nor have we safety in any other way than by permanently abiding in water; so that most monstrous creature, who had no right to teach even sound doctrine, knew full well how to kill the little fishes, by taking them away from the water! (ON BAPTISM, CHAPTER 1)

ΙΧΘΥΣ is the Greek word for fish, and the letters are understood as an acrostic for Jesus:

Ι—Jesus

Χ—Christ

Θ—God's

Υ—Son

Σ—Savior

From the early days of the New Testament Church, the symbol of the fish has been one of the marks of a Christian. Tertullian reminds us what this means: we live in the water. The devil, "that most monstrous creature," knows how to destroy the fish, by taking them away from the gifts and promises God gives in the Gospel and delivers in Baptism.

The devil attacks repentance. He attacks the preaching of the Law. He attacks the preaching of the Gospel. He attacks the truth that Jesus is the Savior. He attacks this by convincing you that you don't need saving, or by convincing you that you can't possibly be saved.

Rage as he does, the devil and his lies cannot destroy this beautiful and comforting truth, this unwavering promise:

Jesus is the Savior.

Jesus is *your* Savior.

This world's prince may still scowl fierce as he will. He can harm us none. He's judged. The deed is done. This one little word can fell him.

10

The Armor of God

Put on the whole armor of God, that you may be able
to stand against the schemes of the devil.

(Ephesians 6:11)

One of the most important texts about spiritual warfare is Ephesians 6:10–18, where Paul commends to us the "whole armor of God." We'll use this passage to answer the question, What is our equipment for war? Along the way, Paul will also answer the question, What is our aim and place in the fight?

Ephesians is a beautiful epistle written by St. Paul from his Roman imprisonment. He writes back to the Christians and the churches he helped establish in Ephesus, perhaps the biggest and most important city in Asia. Paul reminds them of the Gospel, of the gift of repentance and faith, of the doctrine of justification. "By grace you have been saved through faith," he reminds them. "And this [faith] is not your own doing; it is the gift of God, not a result of works, so that no one may boast" (2:8–9). He also reminds these saints that "we are His workmanship, created in Christ Jesus for good works, which God prepared beforehand, that we should walk in them" (2:10). These good works take shape according to the Ten Commandments and according to our various vocations and callings. Paul, in Ephesians 5:22–6:9, provides a "table of

71

duties," showing how the Christian faith enlivens husbands and wives, parents and children, bond servants and masters.

This is important context for the passage we will consider. Paul is describing a soldier who is on guard duty, and each one of us is stationed in our vocations. If we are parents, we are stationed in our homes to do spiritual guard duty for our children. If we are pastors in a congregation, we are stationed there to do spiritual guard duty for the families of the congregation. Christians are in their cities and neighborhoods as spiritual sentries.

In the ancient world, the Romans placed sentries all along their borders. Those soldiers were to stand night and day, alert, watching for danger. If there was any trouble that they could see or hear, they would call in the reinforcements, shouting or blowing a trumpet. They were not to fight on their own—that would be futile. Their job was to stand, to stay awake, to stay alert, to watch, to listen, and to call for help when needed.

It is helpful to picture yourself standing on the wall of a great city. Everyone in the city is sleeping, but you are there, looking out, scanning the horizon, watching, listening, noting the movements of the enemy, and reporting them to your commanding officer. This is our duty in spiritual warfare. We stand on the watchtowers of the estates, in the places where the Lord has put us. We watch to see how the enemy attacks, and we pray for the Lord's help.

To keep us safe as we man our posts, the Lord Jesus has given us equipment, spiritual armor.

> **Finally, be strong in the Lord and in the strength of His might. Put on the whole armor of God, that you may be able to stand against the schemes of the devil.** (EPHESIANS 6:10–11)

We are not scheming. We are resisting and standing against the schemes of the devil. The devil is busy and active, working to overthrow the Lord's kingdom. We are still, standing, watching. There is a calmness to the Christian's place in this battle.

> For we do not wrestle against flesh and blood, but
> against the rulers, against the authorities, against the cos-
> mic powers over this present darkness, against the spir-
> itual forces of evil in the heavenly places. (EPHESIANS 6:12)

This verse is key. Who are we fighting? Paul reminds us that our fight is not against flesh and blood, that is, we do not battle against other people. The Christian is not at war with any other human being. We can't be. If our Lord Jesus has died for all (see 2 Corinthians 5:14), if God is in Christ reconciling the world to Himself (2 Corinthians 5:19), then how can we be at war with them? How can the Christian be at war with a person for whom Christ died?

We, then, are not authorized to consider any other person to be our enemy. Other people, no doubt, will consider *us* to be *their* enemy. In those circumstances, we know what to do. We have our marching orders from Jesus: "Love your enemies and pray for those who persecute you" (Matthew 5:44).

Our battles are spiritual. We are not fighting flesh and blood. We are fighting against the demons, "the rulers, against the authorities, against the cosmic powers over this present darkness, against the spiritual forces of evil in the heavenly places." Our equipment is spiritual equipment.

> For though we walk in the flesh, we are not waging war
> according to the flesh. For the weapons of our warfare are
> not of the flesh but have divine power to destroy strong-
> holds. (2 CORINTHIANS 10:3–4)

Paul also gives us fantastic clarity regarding success. What does it mean to finish the fight, to conquer? It means, at the end of our life and the end of the world, we are still standing. Listen to all the "standing" we are set to do:

> Therefore take up the whole armor of God, that you
> may be able to withstand in the evil day, and having done
> all, to stand firm. Stand therefore . . ." (EPHESIANS 6:13–14)

Withstand . . . stand . . . stand. We are not to charge. We are not to attack. We are not summoned to rush into battle. Like a sentry standing on the wall, we stand, we watch, and we pray.

Much of the conversation about spiritual warfare has the Christian marching out to war, going out to fight, taking territory from the devil. That is not the picture St. Paul puts before us. We are on guard duty. We stand.

(There is one exception to this in the list of equipment: the shoes of readiness. We'll talk about that later.)

You can almost picture Paul in his prison cell in Rome, looking at the soldier guarding him, his uniform and equipment, and seeing the parallel between the soldier's armor and the gifts the Holy Spirit gives to Christians in their Baptism: the equipment for the battle, the armor of God.

We will be tempted to read this list of equipment as things we are to do or accomplish on our own. This is not the case. This equipment is provided by the Lord. They are His gifts.

First, the belt of truth.

Stand therefore, having fastened on the belt of truth . . .
(EPHESIANS 6:14A)

Christians are truth-tellers. We have a profound interest in the truth of things and in the personal integrity that always seeks and speaks the truth. The belt of truth, though, is not our own truth telling, but the truth which God speaks to us.

We reject outright the idea that there is no truth, or that truth cannot be known, or that each person has their own truth. There is a truth of things, a truth of history, a truth of justice. This belt, though, is not the belt of just any truth. It is the belt of the truth of Jesus.

Jesus says, "I am the way, and the truth, and the life. No one comes to the Father except through Me" (John 14:6). The Christian truth is a person, Jesus Christ. His person, His work, His Word—these are the belt with which we are girded. The very first piece of spiritual armor is confidence in the simple truth of the Scriptures: Jesus is Lord.

Next, the breastplate of righteousness.

> . . . and having put on the breastplate of righteous-
> ness . . . (EPHESIANS 6:14B)

The breastplate protects the heart. Again, this protection is not provided by our own works and efforts. It is not our own righteousness that keeps us safe! This is not a breastplate of our works stitched together with our own paltry acts. Can you imagine that breastplate, full of holes, falling apart, miserable, and not at all safe? No, this breastplate is the impenetrable righteousness of the Lord Jesus Christ.

Remember the great exchange of the Gospel. Jesus took upon Himself our sins in order to give us His righteousness. His suffering was for our atonement. The chastisement for our sin was put on Him (Isaiah 53:5).

> For our sake He made Him to be sin who knew no sin,
> so that in Him we might become the righteousness of God.
> (2 CORINTHIANS 5:21)

We should not miss the almost unimaginable glory of that passage. First, that Jesus, the holy and eternal Son of God, was made sin. Second, that He was made sin for us! Third, that the purpose of His being made sin was that we would be made righteous. And, fourth, that the righteousness won for us is none other than the righteousness of God! God's perfection, God's holiness, the perfect keeping of the Law that Jesus fulfilled, is given to you by faith in the Gospel so that the Lord Jesus considers you a partaker in His own righteousness. By faith, you are as holy, perfect, and righteous as Jesus is!

No wonder Paul warns us of the dangers of seeking a righteousness of our own works and efforts. A righteousness of our own could only come from the Law, but we have a righteousness "which comes through faith in Christ, the righteousness from God that depends on faith" (Philippians 3:9).

That righteousness, the righteousness of Christ given through the Gospel, is the righteousness with which we are equipped. We are clothed with Christ! (See Galatians 3:27 and especially Romans 13:14, noting the context of Romans 13:12.) Our hearts are safe, protected from the demons with the Lord's righteousness and His "armor of light" (Romans 13:12).

Next, our feet.

> . . . and, as shoes for your feet, having put on the readiness given by the gospel of peace. (Ephesians 6:15)

Here is the one exception to standing: we are shod with the shoes of readiness. We are supposed to run.

The picture here is of a messenger, the soldier who runs from the battle back to town to announce the results of the battle.

This is how marathons started, at least according to the ancient legend. The Greeks were fighting the Persians at Marathon (in the year 490 BC). After an important victory, Pheidippides, a runner, covered the twenty-five miles from Marathon to Athens, gave the announcement "Rejoice! We won!" and then dropped dead on the spot.

You can imagine the importance of these runners. The soldiers have gone off to battle. There is no TV news, no embedded reporters, no way to know what is happening. You can see the smoke rising over the horizon. You can hear the distant sounds of war, but you don't know how it's going. You don't know who has won. You don't know if your husband and son will march back over the horizon or if it will be your enemies coming for you. You wait anxiously for the runner to come with news—either the bad news, "We lost, run for the hills!" or the good news, "Rejoice! We won!"

The Greek word for *Gospel* comes out of this context. It means "good news," the announcement of victory. The Christian Gospel is the announcement of a very specific Good News, that Jesus has won. He has prevailed over sin, death, and the devil. He endured the wrath of God, the forsakenness of God, the shame and agony of the crucifixion, and He has prevailed. Jesus has won the victory, and He sends this Good News to the world through the prophets and the apostles, through preachers and teachers.

"Rejoice! Christ is risen! Salvation has come! Jesus is Lord! The war is over. We are at peace with God."

Paul unfolds this beautifully in Romans 10:13–15:

> For "everyone who calls on the name of the Lord will be saved."
>
> How then will they call on Him in whom they have not believed? And how are they to believe in Him of whom they have never heard? And how are they to hear without someone preaching? And how are they to preach unless they are sent? As it is written, "How beautiful are the feet of those who preach the good news!"

The beautiful feet belong to the messenger who carries the good news of victory from the battle to the people. The messenger proclaims peace!

The shoes included in the armor of God are the shoes of readiness to run and announce this Good News. Every Christian, then, is not only a hearer of the Good News but also a speaker of that same news. We announce the victory of Jesus over sin, death, and the devil wherever we find ourselves. Our feet have put on the readiness given by the gospel of peace.

We also have a shield.

> In all circumstances take up the shield of faith, with which you can extinguish all the flaming darts of the evil one. (EPHESIANS 6:16)

Faith is the shield with which the devil's darts are extinguished.

This verse, at first, is a bit of a shock. "Wait," we say, "the devil is shooting fiery arrows at us?!" Indeed. These are his spiritual attacks, his temptations, his maneuvers meant to undermine our repentance. Most of the time, we don't even know that we are being shot at. We are like blindfolded people crossing the street, ignorant of our constant danger.

The shield of faith is there, stopping the flaming arrows and deadly darts.

What is this faith? The Bible speaks of faith in two ways: the faith that is believed and the faith that believes. The first, the faith that is believed, is the doctrine, the teaching, the content of the Gospel. The second, the faith that believes, is the trust and confidence of the Christian in this teaching and preaching. These two always go together.

We are in danger of thinking of faith always as our subjective trust, as our believing, and we forget that the strength of faith is in its object. Our faith saves not because of the strength of the faith but on the strength of the object of our faith.

Here's an illustration. Imagine two men come to a frozen river. One has very strong faith in the ice, and he drives his snowmobile right across. The other man has very weak faith in the ice. He crawls very slowly and carefully across the river. Both men make it to the other side, not because their faith was strong or weak, but because the river was frozen solid.

They come back two weeks later. The man with strong faith drives his snowmobile onto the ice, crashes through, and sinks to the bottom of the river. The other man gets halfway across before the ice below him breaks, and he also falls in. Both men fell into the river, not because of their faith (or lack of faith), but because the ice was paper thin.

So it is with faith. It is not the strength of our faith but the object of our faith that matters. The shield of faith we bear is the confession of Jesus the Savior. It is strong not because our faith is rock-solid but because Jesus is risen and ascended. It quenches the flaming darts of the devil not because we hold it so steady but because it is saturated with the sin-forgiving blood of Jesus.

We also have headgear, the helmet of salvation.

. . . and take the helmet of salvation . . . (EPHESIANS 6:17A)

The helmet protects the head. Our mind, our thoughts, our imagination, our study, our convictions, our reason, our plans—all of these are guarded by the salvation that is ours in Christ.

We note again that this salvation is not our own doing. It is the work of Christ. Jesus is the Savior. We are the saved. It is the saving work of Christ that also protects our head.

Some Christians are tempted to disconnect the life of the mind with their life of faith. This is dangerous and wrong. Jesus says, "Love the Lord your God with all your heart and with all your soul and with all your mind and with all your strength" (Mark 12:30). Our mind is an important part of our Christian life of faith, love, and hope, and when Paul equips us with the helmet of salvation, he reminds us that the foundation of our thoughts and the regular object of our reflection is the salvation won for us through the death and resurrection of Jesus.

Our minds, then, are not anxious about God's wrath; we are not afraid of death, we are not scheming to sin or planning our attempts to get into heaven by our efforts. All of this has been accomplished. With these things settled, we are free to think and imagine, to study this cosmos and reflect on how we might bless and serve our neighbor.

In another letter, Paul speaks of the armor of God using a slightly different picture. In that place, he expands on the use of the helmet of salvation:

> But since we belong to the day, let us be sober, having put on the breastplate of faith and love, and for a helmet the hope of salvation. For God has not destined us for wrath, but to obtain salvation through our Lord Jesus Christ, who died for us so that whether we are awake or asleep we might live with Him. Therefore encourage one another and build one another up, just as you are doing.
> (1 THESSALONIANS 5:8–11)

Paul connects the helmet of salvation with hope. We set our minds not only on the things the Lord has done for us but also on the things to come that the Lord has promised. Salvation is the forgiveness of our sins, but it doesn't stop there. Salvation is dying in the faith and coming to the beautiful vision of God, seeing Jesus face-to-face. Salvation is the resurrection on the Last Day and attaining the resurrection from the dead, the eternal life of the new heaven and new earth where righteousness dwells. Salvation is being rescued from this valley of tears, from this life of trouble and all the assaults of the devil, the world, and the flesh.

Salvation is ours now, with more to come! Life will give way to more life. Hope, as opposed to fear and despair, is the mark of the Christian mind. We'll say much more about hope in the next major section. It is enough to note here that the hope of salvation protects, guards, and even governs our thoughts. For those who are in Christ Jesus, there is an eternal life in and of the mind.

Finally, Paul gives us the single piece of offensive equipment, the sword of the Spirit.

> . . . and [take up] the sword of the Spirit, which is the word of God, praying at all times in the Spirit, with all prayer and supplication. (EPHESIANS 6:17–18)

The Roman soldiers were known for their deft handling of their short swords. Would that the Christian Church would have the same reputation for handling the Word of truth!

The Word of God is the Spirit's sword, the Spirit's Word. The Holy Spirit spoke by the prophets and apostles, so we have a great confidence that the words of the Bible are the true, infallible, life-giving words of the Holy Spirit.

When we consider that the devil tempts us with lying words, then it fits that it is with words of truth that we mount the counterattack.

Jesus is our exemplar. After His Baptism, He was driven into the wilderness to be tempted by the devil. Jesus addresses and rebuffs each temptation not with His divine strength or majesty but with the Lord's Word. "Turn this stone to bread," the devil says. Jesus responds with Deuteronomy 8:3, "It is written, 'Man shall not live by bread alone, but by every word that comes from the mouth of God'" (Matthew 4:4).

In round two, the devil comes with the Scriptures, misquoted and misapplied. "Jump off the temple," he says, "and the Lord will send His angels to protect You." The devil quotes Psalm 91:11–12, but he leaves out a key part of the passage.

Here is the entire text from the psalm:

> For He will command His angels concerning you
>   to guard you in all your ways.
> On their hands they will bear you up,
>   lest you strike your foot against a stone.

The devil took out "in all your ways." The Lord doesn't promise us protection and safety in whatever it is that we want to do. He doesn't promise to cause us to float to the ground if we jump from the top of a mountain. He doesn't promise to stop a train if we jump in front of it. His provision is promised as we live out our vocations, as we walk in the ways that He has put in front of us.

The devil wants to misapply this promise to Jesus and thus cause Jesus to tempt the Lord. Jesus' response, from Deuteronomy 6:16, is perfect. "Again it is written, 'You shall not put the Lord your God to the test'" (Matthew 4:7).

Finally, the devil shows Jesus all the kingdoms of the world and says, "Worship me, and I'll give all these to You." This is a confusing temptation. It seems the least likely to succeed, but it does show the devil's strategy and his deepest desire. He wants to be worshiped, by us and by God. He wants to be exalted above all others.

He offers Jesus the world without the cross if Jesus will only worship him. Jesus again responds with the Scriptures, Deuteronomy 6:13 and 1 Samuel 7:3: "Be gone, Satan! For it is written, 'You shall worship the Lord your God and Him only shall you serve'" (Matthew 4:10).

The devil left Him, and the angels came and comforted Him.

Jesus used "the sword of the Spirit which is the word of God." We have that same sword.

We see the devil's strategy on display in the temptation of Jesus.

First, the devil uses words. He comes with bad doctrine, bad ideas, lies and half-truths. He is a liar. The battle with the devil is a war of words.

Second, the devil uses our own desires against us. (We'll consider this much more in the fourth section of the book.) Jesus had not eaten in forty days. He was hungry, and the devil comes along and says, "You're hungry. I'll help You. I want what You want. Turn this stone into bread. I'm Your friend. I want You to be full and satisfied. And, it turns out, God is the bad guy. He doesn't want You to have what You want."

Third, the devil misuses God's Word. The devil knows the Bible, and he twists it to fit his ends. He gives us the Law when we need Gospel and the Gospel when we need Law. Before we sin, when he is tempting us, he preaches a perverted gospel: "Don't worry; God won't get mad. God is love." Then, if we sin, he brings a twisted law: "You call yourself a Christian? God can never love you." The devil misuses the Gospel to excuse sin, and the Law to damn the sinner. Jesus, on the other hand, wants us to look back with the Gospel (knowing that our sins are forgiven) and forward with the Law (considering how we are to love the Lord and our neighbor).

Fourth, the devil offers ways for us to avoid suffering. "I'll give You these kingdoms without the cross," he says to Jesus. What a friendly devil! He doesn't want us to suffer, so he'll provide a shortcut, a broad and easy way for us to walk.

In all of these things, the devil acts like our friend, even our savior. He decks himself in light (see 2 Corinthians 11:14). His enmity is most often hidden, and he wants to set us at war with God.

It was no different in the beginning. The devil came to Adam and Eve as a friend. "Look at this nice fruit. You want it, and I want you to have it. You know who doesn't? God, and it's because He knows that if you eat it you will be like Him. He's jealous. He's petty. He wants control over you. Not me; I want you to be free." See how the devil turns everything on its head?

But where Adam and Eve fell, Jesus stood. Jesus resisted temptation. He stood against the devil. He stood for you and me.

We rejoice in this in two ways. First, we see that Jesus was in the wilderness for us. He was fighting the devil for us. He was tempted in our stead. He stood where Adam and Eve fell. He is our champion, and in the wilderness, He was fighting and overcoming the devil—an overcoming that will extend through the cross and culminate on the Last Day. Second, we rejoice that Jesus shows us how to fight the devil. The devil's attacks are to be resisted not by mustering great spiritual strength but by taking up the Word of God.

When we think of the Scriptures, we think about how they are inspired and true. Especially when we think of the Reformation and the teaching of *sola Scriptura* ("Scripture alone"), we think of how the Bible is the teaching authority in the church. All these things are true, but the Word of God is even more. It is our sword, our chief weapon for the spiritual battle.

Perhaps no one in the church understood this better than Martin Luther. Consider these passages from the Large Catechism where Luther encourages us to stand against the devil in the strength of God's Word:

> Besides, catechism study is a most effective help against the devil, the world, the flesh, and all evil thoughts. It helps to be occupied with God's Word, to speak it, and meditate on it, just as the first Psalm declares people blessed who meditate on God's Law day and night (Psalm 1:2). Certainly you will not release a stronger incense or other repellent against the devil than to be engaged by God's commandments and words, and speak, sing, or think them. For this is indeed the true "holy water" and "holy sign" from which the devil runs and by which he may be driven away. (PREFACE, 10)

> The devil is called the master of a thousand arts. But what shall we call God's Word, which drives away and brings to nothing this master of a thousand arts with all his arts and power? The Word must indeed be the master of more than a hundred thousand arts. And shall we easily despise such power, profit, strength, and fruit—we, especially, who claim to be pastors and preachers? (PREFACE, 12–13)

> Clearly [God the Father] did not solemnly require and command this [meditation on His Word] without a purpose. For He knows our danger and need, as well as the constant and furious assaults and temptations of devils. He wants to warn, equip, and preserve us against them, as with a good armor against their fiery darts and with good medicine against their evil infection and temptation. Oh, what mad, senseless fools are we! While we must ever live and dwell among such mighty enemies as the devils, we

still despise our weapons and defense, and we are too lazy to look at or think of them! (PREFACE, 14–15)

Let me tell you this, even though you know God's Word perfectly and are already a master in all things: you are daily in the devil's kingdom. He ceases neither day nor night to sneak up on you and to kindle in your heart unbelief and wicked thoughts against these three commandments and all the commandments. Therefore, you must always have God's Word in your heart, upon your lips, and in your ears. But where the heart is idle and the Word does not make a sound, the devil breaks in and has done the damage before we are aware. On the other hand, the Word is so effective that whenever it is seriously contemplated, heard, and used, it is bound never to be without fruit. It always awakens new understanding, pleasure, and devoutness and produces a pure heart and pure thoughts. For these words are not lazy or dead, but are creative, living words. And even though no other interest or necessity moves us, this truth ought to urge everyone to the Word, because thereby the devil is put to flight and driven away. Besides, this commandment is fulfilled and this exercise in the Word is more pleasing to God than any work of hypocrisy, however brilliant. (THIRD COMMANDMENT, 100–102)

It is stunning for us to consider that the devil always attacks the Word, but it is the Word with which we attack him! He throws himself against the wall of God's Word. He is like the moth that is drawn to the flame that will destroy him.

One more word about the sword of the Spirit, regarding how it is to be wielded. This is often missed in the text. Paul says, "[Take up] the sword of the Spirit, which is the word of God, praying at all times in the Spirit, with all prayer and supplication. To that end, keep alert with all perseverance, making supplication for all the saints" (Ephesians 6:17–18). We wield the sword of the Spirit in prayer.

We take up God's Word in order to speak and pray it back to Him. We look for the promises of God and ask Him to keep them with us. We look for the commands of God and ask God to give us His Spirit so that we would begin to keep them. We look for the wisdom of God and ask that we could serve and bless our neighbors with that wisdom. We look for the things that God has instituted, and we pray that He would protect them.

We stand guard in our vocations, with one ear open to the troubles in this world and one ear open to the voice of God. We know the difficulties of this life, and we know the promises of God, and we mix these up together in our prayers.

A wise pastor once told me, "The devil can twist everything you do and say and use it against you. Everything but prayer. When we pray, the Lord hears our prayers, He perfects them, and He answers them perfectly." When we take up the sword of the Spirit in our prayers, we are standing against the devil, armed, safe, and dangerous to the darkness that is around us.

The night is far gone; the day is at hand. So then let us cast off the works of darkness and put on the armor of light. (ROMANS 13:12)

11

The Cross Is the Devil's Defeat

Now is the judgment of this world;
now will the ruler of this world be cast out.

(JOHN 12:31)

The battle that began in the Garden of Eden ended on Golgotha. "It is finished!" This was Jesus' victory shout (John 19:30). Jesus triumphed over sin. Jesus triumphed over death. Jesus triumphed over the devil.

The consistent testimony of the Scriptures is that the death of Jesus is the devil's destruction.

The reason the Son of God appeared was to destroy the works of the devil. (1 JOHN 3:8B)

He disarmed the rulers and authorities and put them to open shame, by triumphing over them in [the cross].
(COLOSSIANS 2:15)

These passages are a great comfort for Christians.

Jesus talks about the devil's defeat in the context of His earthly ministry. When Jesus sends out seventy disciples to preach and deliver the people from the demons, they return rejoicing. Jesus says, "I saw Satan fall like lightning from heaven" (Luke 10:18).

In John 12, Jesus is getting the people ready for the death He is about to die. He prays, "Father, glorify Your name." God the Father answers this prayer, "I have glorified it, and I will glorify it again" (v. 28). The people hear the voice but cannot discern what it is. Some think it is the voice of an angel, others thunder, but Jesus explains it:

> This voice has come for your sake, not Mine. Now is the judgment of this world; now will the ruler of this world be cast out. And I, when I am lifted up from the earth, will draw all people to Myself. (JOHN 12:30–32)

Notice the words used so far. The works of the devil are "destroyed." He is "disarmed" and "triumphed over." He "fell" and is "judged" and "cast out."

This being cast out is unfolded beautifully for us in Revelation 12, the vision of the war in heaven, which we considered earlier. The devil has been stripped of his accusing authority by the blood of Christ. The devil has been removed from his place, his office, by the atoning work and sacrifice of Jesus.

Jesus unfolds all of this wonderful teaching in the parable of the strong man.

Here's the context. As Jesus was traveling around preaching the kingdom of God, He was also rescuing people from troubles, diseases, and the demons. The Pharisees, who were setting up to oppose Jesus at every turn, saw that He was casting out demons, and they accused Him of being possessed, of casting out demons with demons.

> And He called them to Him and said to them in parables, "How can Satan cast out Satan? If a kingdom is divided against itself, that kingdom cannot stand. And if a house is divided against itself, that house will not be able to stand. And if Satan has risen up against himself and is divided, he cannot stand, but is coming to an end. But no one can enter a strong man's house and plunder his goods, unless he first binds the strong man. Then indeed he may plunder his house." (MARK 3:23–27; SEE ALSO MATTHEW 12:29–30)

The little one-sentence parable of the stronger man is what we are after. The strong man is the devil. His house is this world, and his goods are all sinners born into his kingdom of darkness. This is a terrible picture. We are the devil's goods.

Luke records more of the details from Jesus' parable. "When a strong man, fully armed, guards his own palace, his goods are safe" (Luke 11:21). The devil is armed, and when he rules, there is a demonic peace. When the devil has someone, he doesn't trouble them. This explains why the wicked always seem to prosper (see Job 21:16; Psalm 73:3; Jeremiah 12:1).

But the parable continues. There is a stronger man, Jesus. "When one stronger than he attacks him and overcomes him, he takes away his armor in which he trusted and divides his spoil" (Luke 11:22). Jesus, in His ministry—in His teaching, healing, and casting out the demons—is disarming and binding the devil and looting his house. We are the loot!

**He has delivered us from the domain of darkness
and transferred us to the kingdom of His beloved Son,
in whom we have redemption, the forgiveness of sins.**
(Colossians 1:13–14)

It is quite wonderful to think of the evangelical work of the Lord's Church in terms of looting the kingdom of the devil. The strong man is bound, and bound for this specific purpose: he can no longer deceive the nations. His death grip on the pagan world has been broken.

Revelation 20 gives us the spiritual view of the binding of the devil. John sees a great angel with a chain and a key. This angel "seized the dragon, that ancient serpent, who is the devil and Satan, and bound him for a thousand years, and threw him into the pit, and shut it and sealed it over him, so that he might not deceive the nations any longer, until the thousand years were ended" (Revelation 20:2–3).

The thousand years, according to the text, begins with the binding of the devil. When did that occur? According to the parable of the stronger man, the devil is bound by the life and death of Jesus. We are, then, living in the time of the thousand years, the time when the Lord's Word and forgiveness and mercy and Church goes out to all the world.

Here's the picture that helps me imagine this. You might have seen the satellite pictures of the world at night. You can see where the people live, where the cities are, by all the lights. The east coast of the United States is a line of light. The wilderness and deserts of the world have very few lights, and the ocean is black.

Let's take this picture, but instead of the lights being where people live, let the light be where people believe the Gospel. Imagine a light map of faith. Now imagine it during the times of the Old Testament. In the days of Abraham, there are a few little lights—Abraham, Lot, Job—but most of the world is darkness. Imagine this map during the time of King David with a little light in Jerusalem, but most of the rest of the world is dark. Imagine the time of Jesus—a little glimmer in Jerusalem, in Bethlehem, in Nazareth, perhaps a little glimmer from the faithful in exile, in Egypt and Babylon, faint lights in a very dark world. But then consider the Book of Acts. The lights start to come on in Jerusalem, then all of Judea, then down to Samaria, to Egypt, to Caesarea, Antioch, Lystra, Derbe, Philippi, then all of Macedonia, then into Greece, Thessalonica, Berea, Athens, Corinth—and we are just tracking Paul. The disciples were carrying the light of the Gospel into all different corners of the world. Soon there would be Christians in India and the Far East, in the Persian and Middle Eastern empires, in Africa, in Asia Minor and all of Asia, into Rome and even past the edges of the Roman Empire into northern Europe.

Paul can already say in his ministry that the Gospel has gone out into all the earth:

> **Of this you have heard before in the word of the truth, the gospel, which has come to you, as indeed in the whole world it is bearing fruit and increasing—as it also does among you, since the day you heard it and understood the grace of God in truth.** (COLOSSIANS 1:5–6; SEE ALSO ROMANS 10:18)

But how can these things be? How can we possibly think that the devil is bound? It seems like five minutes of reading the newspaper or listening to the evening news indicates that the devil is loose and free, that his kingdom is flourishing and his reign is increasing.

Hebrews 2 is key.

We start with verses 14–15.

> Since therefore the children share in flesh and blood, He Himself likewise partook of the same things, that through death He might destroy the one who has the power of death, that is, the devil, and deliver all those who through fear of death were subject to lifelong slavery.

We are flesh and blood, mortal human beings. Jesus partook of the same, became a true man in the incarnation. He needed flesh and blood so that He could suffer and die. This is truly stunning. Jesus is true man so that He could truly be tempted, truly suffer, truly die and be buried. And, this text tells us, the result of His death is the destruction of the devil. Through His death, Jesus destroyed the devil. What wonderful and fantastic news! But the problem remains: we don't see it.

Hebrews 2:7–9 answers this problem, beginning with a quotation from Psalm 8, where King David was singing and praying about the humiliation and exaltation of the coming Messiah:

> You made Him for a little while lower than the angels; you have crowned Him with glory and honor, putting everything in subjection under His feet.

The author of the Book of Hebrews expounds on the Old Testament text.

> Now in putting everything in subjection to Him, He left nothing outside His control. At present, we do not yet see everything in subjection to Him. But we see Him who for a little while was made lower than the angels, namely Jesus, crowned with glory and honor because of the suffering of death, so that by the grace of God He might taste death for everyone.

All things are under the feet of Jesus. We don't see it yet.

Jesus has destroyed the devil. We don't see it yet.

Jesus has destroyed our death, our grave, our sin. We don't see it yet.

But, the text reminds us, we do see Jesus in His humility. We know of the death and resurrection of Jesus. We do know of His suffering and sacrifice, and this is enough for us now, to walk by faith and not by sight (2 Corinthians 5:7). The triumph and reign of Jesus is hidden from our eyes and revealed only to our ears.

Here's the picture. When we were kids, my brothers and I would always count the time between lightning and thunder. You could tell how far away the lightning strike was by the gap between what you saw and what you heard. I'm pretty sure our accuracy was questionable! Because light and sound travel at different speeds, the vision and the sound of the same event reach you at different times.

This is the way it is with the victory of Jesus on the cross, only reversed. The sound reaches us before the sight. The preaching gets to our ears before the reality unfolds before our eyes. We live in the gap between the thunder of the Gospel and the lightning flash of the second coming.

This includes, according to Hebrews 2, the triumph of Jesus over the devil. We hear it. We don't see it, but we know the Scriptures are true. We know the devil is defeated, his works are destroyed, his kingdom is in ruins, and one day soon we will see this triumph with our own eyes.

12

They Did Not Love
Their Lives unto Death

*What are you doing, weeping and
breaking my heart? For I am ready not
only to be imprisoned but even to die in
Jerusalem for the name of the Lord Jesus.*

(Acts 21:13)

We've been focusing on Jesus and His work to overcome and overthrow the devil. We now will consider what this means for us.

Jesus, after all, is on a rescue mission. We are the rescued. He doesn't take up the battle against the devil for His own sake but for ours. He binds the strong man in order to take his stuff, to get us back. He fights the devil for us, for our benefit. His victory is our rescue and our freedom.

We've considered both Revelation 12 and Hebrews 2. Revelation 12 gives us the vision of the heavenly throne room and the expulsion of the accuser from that court. Hebrews 2 explains the mystery of the devil's unseen defeat. An important theme runs through both texts that we want to consider now: the fear of death.

As Hebrews 2 unfolds the victory of Jesus over the devil, it also gives us insight into the devil's work.

> Since therefore the children share in flesh and blood, He
> Himself likewise partook of the same things, that through
> death He might destroy the one who has the power of death,
> that is, the devil, and deliver all those who through fear
> of death were subject to lifelong slavery. (HEBREWS 2:14–15)

Notice, now, how this text describes the power of the devil: "the one who has the power of death, that is, the devil." This does not mean that the devil has the power to kill or murder us. Our lives are in the Lord's hands, and the devil can only take what the Lord gives (see Matthew 10:29–31; Psalm 139:16; 1 Samuel 2:6; and remember Job 1:12 and 2:6). What does it mean, then, that the devil "has the power of death"? This is explained in verse 15: "those who through fear of death were subject to lifelong slavery." The power of death is the fear of death. And, let's say this as clearly as possible, the fear of death is a demonic bondage.

We all will admit that death is scary. When we imagine death, our own or the death of a loved one, it knocks us around a bit. It takes the wind out of us. We don't want to die, and each of us knows, deep down, that we are not supposed to die. God created us to live, to have life and joy without end. While we know instinctively that death is bad, the Bible tells us even more. Death is the punishment for sin. Paul reminds us of the curse: "The wages of sin is death" (Romans 6:23). And there is more. Judgment waits for us on the other side of death. "It is appointed for man to die once, and after that comes judgment" (Hebrews 9:27). Our conscience constantly reminds us of our guilt, and it all piles up at the point of death.

We all, then, have a natural fear of death. We are afraid of what might be on the other side of death. If it's nothing or if it's something, it all seems bad to us.

In some ways, the fear of death is helpful. It helps keep us alive; it keeps us from recklessness and foolishness. There is wisdom, even, in knowing that our days are numbered (see Psalm 90:11–12). Recognizing our own mortality is simply being aware of what makes us human.

But the devil comes along and pushes an awareness of death to the point of fear. He uses our dying against us. The devil uses the fear of death to bind us, to keep us, according to Hebrews 2, in "lifelong slavery." We see how this works. When we fear death, we are open to manipulation. "If you do that good thing, you will die. If you don't do this bad thing, I'll kill you."

We see this temptation most acutely with the ancient martyrs. The Romans had declared Christianity illegal, and Christians especially were accused of rebellion because they refused to say "Caesar is Lord" and offer the sacrifice of a pinch of incense to the Caesar cult. "It is not much to ask," the prosecutor would say. "And if you refuse, you die." Thus the devil would use the fear of death to force a denial of the Lord Jesus.

It's an old story. Shadrach, Meshach, and Abednego were told to worship the golden image or be thrown into the fire (Daniel 3). Daniel had the option of ceasing his prayers or being thrown to the lions (Daniel 6). The devil loves to set it up this way: sin or die.

For us, it is subtler most of the time. The devil puts little deaths before us. Lie or lose your job. Cheat or lose your grade. Say nothing or lose your friendship. Change your conviction or lose your status. Whatever it is—the fear of death, the fear of loss, the fear of shame—fear is sitting behind the devil's threat. When we are afraid, he's got us tied up.

Fear is worship, at least part of worship. This is why the commandment "You shall have no other gods" is explained "We should fear, love, and trust in God above all things" (Small Catechism, First Commandment). The Bible is full of references to fear, especially the fear of the Lord. This fear is exclusive. When He says, "Fear Me," He means, "Fear Me alone. Fear Me only." He intends to cast out all other fears.

When suffering or pain says, "You should fear me," we respond, "I fear God."

When loss comes along, or shame, and asks us to be afraid, we say, "I fear God."

When the devil trots up and says, "You should be afraid of me," we say, "Nope, my fear belongs to God."

One thing after another comes along and tempts us to worship with our fear, and the Christian says, "My fear belongs to God."

This is what Jesus is getting at when He says, "I tell you, My friends, do not fear those who kill the body, and after that have nothing more that they can do. But I will warn you whom to fear: fear Him who, after He has killed, has authority to cast into hell. Yes, I tell you, fear Him!" (Luke 12:4–5).

When death comes demanding the worship of fear, we say, "I fear God, God alone. There is no fear left for you." When our fear goes to God, something wonderful happens—actually, three wonderful things. One, there is no fear left for anything else. Two, there is no need to fear anything else, because, three, the Lord turns to us who fear Him and says, "Don't be afraid." Over and over He says it. Jesus says it to the disciples, "Don't be afraid"; to His Church, "Do not fear." When we, at last, fear God, then God comes to us and says, "I'm nothing to be afraid of. I love you. I've redeemed you. You belong to Me. Your life is in My hands. You will live with Me forever. Don't be afraid." This perfect love of God for us casts out fear (see 1 John 4:18).

There is, then, a fearlessness to the Christian life.

> **Do not fear what you are about to suffer. Behold, the devil is about to throw some of you into prison, that you may be tested, and for ten days you will have tribulation. Be faithful unto death, and I will give you the crown of life.** (REVELATION 2:10)

The freedom of the Gospel is a freedom from the fear of death. One day you will die. Because of the death of Jesus, this is nothing to fear. Your sins are forgiven. God's wrath over your sin has been spent on Jesus. Jesus, at this very moment, as you read these words, is preparing a place for you so that where He is, you will be also (John 14:3). Jesus has taken the sting out of death by taking the punishment in your place.

Paul sings the prophets' triumph over death and then adds a stanza of his own:

> **"Death is swallowed up in victory."**
> **"O death, where is your victory?**
> **O death, where is your sting?"**

> The sting of death is sin, and the power of sin is the
> law. But thanks be to God, who gives us the victory through
> our Lord Jesus Christ. (1 CORINTHIANS 15:54–57; SEE ALSO ISAIAH 25:8
> AND HOSEA 13:14)

Paul here shows why death is so fearful. "The sting of death is sin, and the power of sin is the law." Death is so frightful because there is, on the other side of death, an accounting for our sins. Judgment follows death. But Jesus took our judgment; He's been judged already, and He has stood and pronounced you to be righteous, forgiven, holy, fit for eternal life. "There is therefore now no condemnation for those who are in Christ Jesus" (Romans 8:1). Jesus says it this way, busting the myth that Christians will be judged when they die: "Truly, truly, I say to you, whoever hears My word and believes Him who sent Me has eternal life. He does not come into judgment, but has passed from death to life" (John 5:24). Let those words sink in: *He does not come into judgment.* You will not come into judgment. What is there to judge? Which of your sins has escaped the gracious attention of Jesus? Which of your transgressions is too strong for His blood? What portion of God's wrath was held back from Jesus and kept for you? Jesus is the Savior, the one who dies for sinners, the one who died for you: "Our Savior Christ Jesus, who abolished death and brought life and immortality to light through the gospel" (2 Timothy 1:10).

Death is swallowed up in victory, swallowed up by the sacrificial victory of Jesus' cross. Death, because of Jesus, is nothing to fear. Death, because of Jesus, has new sweet and soft names such as "taken away from calamity" (Isaiah 57:1), "sleep" (Matthew 9:24; John 11:11; 1 Thessalonians 4:13; Daniel 12:2), "rest" (Revelation 14:13; Hebrews 4:11), "passed from death to life" (John 5:24), "rescue . . . from every evil" (2 Timothy 4:18), and "gain" (Philippians 1:21).

Imagine it! Because of the death and resurrection of Jesus, our greatest enemy has become the thing that we long for. The Christian's death is the way to life and joy eternal. In this way, when we are not afraid, we are free. Free to die and free to live. Free from the devil's manipulation and coercion.

This is beautifully put forward for us in Revelation 12. After hearing the glorious news that the devil has been removed from the heavenly courtroom, that he is no longer accusing us before the throne of the Father, and that he has come down to the earth in fury, we hear that the saints on earth overcome the devil. They do so with three weapons. This is important.

> **And they have conquered him by the blood of the Lamb and by the word of their testimony, for they loved not their lives even unto death.** (Revelation 12:11)

The devil is overcome by (1) the blood of Jesus, (2) the word of their testimony, and (3) the saints not loving their lives unto death.

First, the precious blood of Jesus is the price paid for our redemption. It is the winning of God's mercy; it is the forgiveness of our sins. It is given to us in the Sacrament of the Altar. Jesus says, "Drink of it, all of you, for this is My blood of the new testament, which is poured out for many for the forgiveness of sins" (see Matthew 26:28 and 1 Corinthians 11:25). His blood justifies us (Romans 5:9), redeems us (Ephesians 1:7), brings us near to Christ and His people (Ephesians 2:13), reconciles us and gives us peace (Colossians 1:20), cleanses us from all sin (1 John 1:7), frees us from our sins (Revelation 1:5), and ransoms us to be the Lord's own people (Revelation 5:9). No wonder it overcomes and conquers the devil (Revelation 12:11).

Second, the Word is the sword of the Spirit that tears down the devil's kingdom. We've noted the irony that the thing the devil attacks is the thing by which he is overcome. We note it again here. The phrase here is "the word of their testimony," or the word of their witness, the word of their martyrdom. This is not the word about them. The word that conquers the devil is the testimony of Jesus (see Revelation 12:17; also Revelation 1:2, 9; 6:9; 11:7; 19:10). But the word and promise and testimony of Jesus are theirs by faith, theirs because they believe it and trust in it. These devil-overcomers believe that the death of Jesus is their life, that the suffering of Jesus is their redemption, that the blood of Jesus is their forgiveness.

Third, they did not love their lives unto death. They were not afraid to die. They did not hold on to their lives as if that were all they had. They knew that there is something more, that what was waiting for them on the other side of death was not judgment or suffering but Jesus and the fullness of the salvation He had won for them. They were not afraid of death—quite the opposite. Their hearts were so gripped with the glorious promises of the resurrection that they welcomed death, even longed for it. They prayed "deliver us from evil," and they looked for that deliverance from this life of sorrow.

"I'll kill you," the devil threatens.

"God be praised!" the martyrs respond. "To live is Christ. To die is gain. It is our desire to depart and be with Christ" (see Philippians 1:21, 23).

We will walk through the valley of the shadow of death, but there is no evil to fear, not when Jesus our Savior is with us. This Christian fearlessness sets us free from the devil's bondage, free to live, free to love, free to risk, free to suffer, free to die, knowing that Jesus has destroyed the works of the devil, and He has done this all for us.

THE
ASSAULT
OF
SUFFERING

POLYCARP: MARTYR. HERO.
ca. AD 156. Smyrna.

Polycarp was bishop in Smyrna at the time of a persecution, and the pagan crowds cried out that Polycarp should be brought before them in the arena. Officials went looking for him. Polycarp wanted to remain in the town, but fellow Christians kept moving him from farm to farm to protect him. Roman soldiers found him, at last, in a small cottage. When they did, he asked that the soldiers be given food if they would give him an hour for undisturbed prayer. He prayed for two hours, for the churches throughout the world.

He was taken into the city on a donkey. The captain of the local troops, a certain Herod, met him and tried to persuade him. "What is the harm in saying 'Caesar is Lord' and offering a pinch of incense? Save yourself." Polycarp was silent. They persisted. He answered, "I won't do it."

Polycarp was eighty-six.

He was brought into the arena, and legend tells that he heard a voice from heaven. "Be strong, Polycarp, and play the man."

In the arena, he stood before the proconsul, who also tried to persuade him. "Look how old you are. Swear by Caesar. Change your mind. Say, 'Away with the atheists!'" (The Romans considered the Christians to be atheists, probably because the Christians refused to worship the Roman gods and the Caesar. And I suppose if you have a thousand different gods, one God would seem like none.) But Polycarp didn't miss a beat. He swept his arms around the crowd, indicated all the heathens in the crowd, and said, "Away with the atheists!" This is not what the proconsul wanted.

"Curse Christ," he insisted.

"Eighty-six years I have served Him, and He never did me any wrong. How can I blaspheme my King who saved me?" Polycarp testified.

"Swear by Caesar!"

"I am a Christian. I swear by Christ. If you want me to teach you the faith, tell me when."

"I have wild beasts," the proconsul said.

"Call them."

"I will burn you with fire."

"Your fire lasts for an hour. There is an eternal fire that will burn the wicked," Polycarp preached. "Why do you delay? Do what you will."

The crowds cried for his death. It was announced three times to the crowd, "Polycarp is a Christian." Wood was gathered. They tied his hands behind his back. Polycarp looked up into heaven and prayed.

"Lord God Almighty, Father of Your beloved and blessed Servant Jesus Christ, through whom we have received full knowledge of You . . . I bless You because You have deemed me worthy of this day and hour, to take my part in the number of the martyrs, in the cup of Your Christ for resurrection to eternal life of soul and body in the immortality of the Holy Spirit. . . . For this and for everything I praise You, I bless You, I glorify You, through the eternal and heavenly High Priest, Jesus Christ, Your beloved Servant, through whom be glory to You with Him and the Holy Spirit both now and unto the ages to come. Amen."

Polycarp: Martyr. Hero.

We'll meet in the resurrection.

13

Suffering and the Attack on Hope: In the Rocks with Shallow Roots

As for what was sown on rocky ground, this is the one who hears the word and immediately receives it with joy, yet he has no root in himself, but endures for a while, and when tribulation or persecution arises on account of the word, immediately he falls away.

(MATTHEW 13:20–21)

After the devil comes the world and the trouble of a life of suffering. This is the seed that falls among the rocks. It grows quickly, quicker than the seed that falls on the good soil, but when the sun comes out, the plant withers and dies.

It often happens that sinners hear the preaching of the Gospel, they believe in Jesus, they rejoice in the forgiveness of their sins, they delight in God's Word, but then life gets hard. We suffer. We suffer the normal stuff of living in a fallen world, the sickness and temptation, sorrow and death. Then there is an extra dose of suffering for being a Christian.

In several ways, being a Christian makes life more difficult. You can't go to brunch on Sunday morning; you are expected in church. You can't go along with the jokes in the locker room. You can't embrace the culture's understanding of life, of love, of what is good. To be a Christian is to be an outsider in this sinful world.

Listen carefully to what Jesus teaches us:

> **If the world hates you, know that it has hated Me before it hated you. If you were of the world, the world would love you as its own; but because you are not of the world, but I chose you out of the world, therefore the world hates you.** (JOHN 15:18–19)

By world, Jesus does not mean this globe, the earth we live on. This is not a natural definition, but supernatural. The world is the combined forces of the culture that stand against Jesus and His kingdom. The world is the devil's kingdom of darkness and all the things that go along with it.

John describes the world and the things of this world for us in his first epistle:

> **Do not love the world or the things in the world. If anyone loves the world, the love of the Father is not in him. For all that is in the world—the desires of the flesh and the desires of the eyes and pride of life—is not from the Father but is from the world. And the world is passing away along with its desires, but whoever does the will of God abides forever.** (1 JOHN 2:15–17)

We see what the world is when we see the crowd of people who gathered together to crucify Jesus—Herod, Pilate, the Pharisees and Sadducees, the Jerusalem mob. All these people were enemies of each other, and still they all found a common enemy in Jesus. All the disparate groups of people continue to find an enemy in those who belong to Jesus: the Holy Christian Church.

Our Baptism marks us off from the world. It is an act of sanctification and therefore an act of separation.

Listen to Paul's preaching on Leviticus 26:12 and Isaiah 52:11.

> Do not be unequally yoked with unbelievers. For what partnership has righteousness with lawlessness? Or what fellowship has light with darkness? What accord has Christ with Belial? Or what portion does a believer share with an unbeliever? What agreement has the temple of God with idols? For we are the temple of the living God; as God said,
>
> I will make My dwelling among them and walk among them,
> and I will be their God,
> and they shall be My people.
> Therefore go out from their midst,
> and be separate from them, says the Lord,
> and touch no unclean thing;
> then I will welcome you,
> and I will be a father to you,
> and you shall be sons and daughters to Me,
> says the Lord Almighty. (2 CORINTHIANS 6:14–18)

The holy cross, marked on our forehead and on our heart, is like a bull's-eye for the world and the devil. The devil sees to it that the world attacks Christians. The devil delights in afflicting the Lord's people.

Jesus warns us about this. "In the world you will have tribulation" (John 16:33). We shouldn't be surprised.

But we are.

We are surprised when we have trouble and sorrow and suffering and pain. Part of the problem is the so-called prosperity gospel. Preachers in this strain, many famous and well-known, lie to Christians and tell them to expect a life of comfort and ease. "Name it and claim it," they say. "God wants you to be rich, healthy, and successful." These are lies, dangerous lies, because they train us to tempt God, to expect from Him things He hasn't promised.

True faith expects God to keep His promises. False faith expects God to keep promises He never made. The devil loves that. He loves for us to expect from God a life of ease because the devil knows that life doesn't exist, and when troubles come, we are disappointed in God.

But it is not only the prosperity preachers who trouble us. Our own flesh expects a good life, a life without suffering. We are surprised by suffering.

Peter wonders why this is. "Beloved, do not be surprised at the fiery trial when it comes upon you to test you, as though something strange were happening to you. But rejoice insofar as you share Christ's sufferings, that you may also rejoice and be glad when His glory is revealed" (1 Peter 4:12–13). John too. "Do not be surprised, brothers, that the world hates you" (1 John 3:13).

It should be no surprise to us that we suffer. It should be no surprise that the world hates us. We are following after Jesus, and to do so, we have taken up our cross as well (Matthew 16:24–26). Jesus bore the cross *for* us. We carry our cross *with* Him.

We want to set our expectations right. We want to know that persecution will come. And we want to understand how the devil attacks us with suffering.

Remember the seed in the rocks. The sun came out, and the plant died. The devil is trying, through suffering, to kill our faith (with unbelief and doubt), to kill our love (through hate and self-absorption), and to kill our hope (with despair). But there is a mystery in the parable. When Jesus warns us about the seed that falls in the rocks, He notes that the problem is *not* the sun. The problem is something unseen: the roots.

> **As for what was sown on rocky ground, this is the one who hears the word and immediately receives it with joy, yet he has no root in himself, but endures for a while, and when tribulation or persecution arises on account of the word, immediately he falls away.** (MATTHEW 13:20–21)

The problem is not the suffering. The problem is not the persecution and the tribulation. The problem is the shallow root. If the roots of the plants would have been deeper in the soil, then the sun would have been a blessing and benefit; the plant would have grown even more.

This is true for the Christian. Suffering is not the problem; shallow roots are the problem. The Lord intends for us to have roots sunk deep into His Word, anchored to His promises. It is not enough to know a few Christian clichés. A bumper-sticker theology cannot survive the intense heat of persecution. The Lord's Word has to sink down into our minds and hearts and consciences and captivate us.

This is the picture of Psalm 1.

> Blessed is the man . . . [whose] delight is in the law of the LORD, and on His law he meditates day and night. He is like a tree planted by streams of water that yields its fruit in its season, and its leaf does not wither. In all that he does, he prospers. The wicked are not so, but are like chaff that the wind drives away. (PSALM 1:1–4)

That is a stunning contrast. On the one hand, there is a tree by a stream—its roots sunk into the ground, its leaves always green, always bearing fruit at the right season. On the other hand, there is the chaff, the husks beaten off the kernels of wheat. The smallest gust of wind blows them away.

The tree is the one who meditates on the Lord's Word, whose roots reach down for the Lord's wisdom, who is planted firmly in the Lord's promises. When the sun of persecution comes out, this person is ready. This person rejoices.

Let's dig our roots into God's Word for a better understanding of our life of suffering.

14

Job, Suffering, and the Assault on the Preaching of the Altar

In all this Job did not sin
or charge God with wrong.

(JOB 1:22)

Job immediately comes to mind when we think of suffering.

Job had it all—a good family, a good name, riches, and wisdom—and then, in two fell swoops, it was stripped away. The Sabean army came and stole away all his oxen and donkeys, fire fell from heaven and destroyed all the sheep, Chaldean raiders stole his camels, all but four of his servants were killed, and a wind knocked down his son's home and killed his ten sons and daughters (Job 1). The devil struck Job with terrible sores, head to foot, so that his friends found him mourning, sitting on an ash heap, scraping his wounds with a broken piece of pottery (Job 2). "They saw that his suffering was very great" (Job 2:13).

Job is a classic study in suffering, but I'd like to suggest a slightly different reading of this text.[2] Let's consider Job a contest between two competing conversations.

2   I'm thankful to Pastor Warren Graff for this insight into Job.

111

The first is the conversation in heaven. This is where we hear that Job is righteous. "The LORD said to Satan, 'Have you considered My servant Job, that there is none like him on the earth, a blameless and upright man, who fears God and turns away from evil?'" (Job 1:8). Job is declared to be righteous by God. This is the doctrine of justification. Job was, like all of us, a sinner. "All have sinned and fall short of the glory of God" (Romans 3:23), and Job was no exception. His righteousness is an imputed righteousness. Job is righteous and upright by faith because he believed the promise of the Gospel and was looking forward to the deliverance of the promised Messiah. Job, in other words, was a Christian. He was righteous because the Lord declared him to be righteous; he was righteous because of the heavenly conversation.

And how did Job know what God thought of him? How did Job know that the Lord declared him to be righteous and had forgiven him his sins? The sacrifice.

> His sons used to go and hold a feast in the house of each one on his day, and they would send and invite their three sisters to eat and drink with them. And when the days of the feast had run their course, Job would send and consecrate them, and he would rise early in the morning and offer burnt offerings according to the number of them all. For Job said, "It may be that my children have sinned, and cursed God in their hearts." Thus Job did continually.
> (JOB 1:4–5)

Job knew the forgiveness of sins in the sacrifice.

This is a tremendous insight into the theology of the Old Testament. The worship of the Old Testament was centered around the altar and the sacrifices, and we are put off by all the killing and burning and blood. But a preaching happens when the people bring an animal to the altar. They know that the animal, the goat or lamb or bull, didn't sin. They are the ones who sinned, who have offended God, who deserve God's anger. When the animal goes on the altar, the people are to know that God is accepting this death in place of another. God's anger is laid onto the innocent bull or the spotless lamb instead of falling on them. This is a preaching of the substitutionary atonement, a preaching of the work that Jesus would come to do.

The blood of bulls and goats cannot take away sins (Hebrews 10:4). Jesus is the Lamb of God, who takes away the sin of the world (John 1:29). The altars and sacrifices of the Old Testament pointed to Jesus, preached Jesus. They forgave sins because of the coming sacrifice of Jesus.

Job believed this. He knew of the heavenly conversation where his sins were forgiven and he was declared righteous. He knew of this conversation from the evidence of the sacrifice.

The other conversation is the conversation with Job's friends, a conversation directed by the devil. This takes up the majority of the book, and the summary of that conversation is this: Job is a sinner. God is angry with Job. Job's suffering is the proof. All Job's affliction, all his troubles, all the death and mourning, sickness and sorrow are proof that God is angry with Job.

Two competing conversations. Two competing sermons. Two competing doctrines.

On the one hand is the love and mercy of God and the forgiveness of Job's sins preached quietly from the altar. On the other hand is the anger of God over Job's sins preached with a megaphone through Job's suffering. The drama of the book is this: Which one will Job listen to? What will Job know to be true?

In this context, we see how the devil uses suffering. The devil wants to preach to us through our suffering. He wants our suffering to teach us about God—that God hates us or doesn't care about us or is angry with us. The devil wants our suffering to teach us about ourselves and the world—that this world is an unjust and unfair place and that God must not be in charge (if there even is a God). We despairingly think of ourselves as deserving of all the suffering, or pridefully, we imagine that our suffering is unjust or unfair.

Whatever it is, the devil is preaching through our suffering, and his preaching is not the preaching of the Gospel. He does not preach the forgiveness of sins. He does not preach faith, love, and hope. He does not preach the righteousness of the Gospel or the death of Jesus. He does not preach the love of God in Christ. In fact, the devil's sermons in suffering can be boiled down to one sentiment: Jesus does not love you.

It is important to see that the devil tries to use suffering to preach false doctrine. Suffering is his first assault on faith.

This is often presented as a philosophical dilemma, the so-called problem of evil, and it shakes out like this:

- If God is all-loving and all-powerful, then everything would be good and not evil.

- There is evil in the world.

- Therefore, God is not all-loving, or not all-powerful, or not powerful at all.

Many a Christian's faith has withered and died under the heat of this argument, scorched by the sun of suffering. If God loved us, things wouldn't be this bad. If God loved us, this world wouldn't be this ugly. If God loved me, then I wouldn't hurt this much.

It must be that God doesn't love me.

(I'm convinced that this conclusion is so terrifying that most find it easier to believe that there is no God at all rather than to believe in a God who hates them.)

What do we say to this problem? How do we address the problem of evil, or better, how does the Lord address it?

We are convinced that there is comfort in the answer to the why questions. "Why is there suffering? Why am I suffering?" The Lord knows better. He has a better comfort for us. Instead of answering the problem of evil with reason, He answers it with promises.

We see this at the end of Job. The Lord Himself comes to speak with Job. He doesn't explain Job's suffering. He doesn't even say, "Job, the devil did all this, not Me." He lets the question stand. He rebukes Job for being too sure of himself.

"Where were you when I laid the foundations of the earth?" (Job 38:4). "Shall the one who contends with the Almighty correct Him? He who rebukes God, let him answer it" (Job 40:2 NKJV). Then, wonderfully,

He rebukes the devil's preaching in suffering and then brings those preachers into His heavenly forgiveness.

Here are Job's friends who have been trying to convince Job that his suffering means God is angry. Here is Job, clinging for his life to the promise of the sacrifice. Now look at what the Lord says at the end.

> **My anger burns against you and against your two friends, for you have not spoken of Me what is right, as My servant Job has. Now therefore take seven bulls and seven rams and go to My servant Job and offer up a burnt offering for yourselves. And My servant Job shall pray for you, for I will accept his prayer not to deal with you according to your folly. For you have not spoken of Me what is right, as My servant Job has.** (JOB 42:7–8)

The friends of Job, at the end, are brought to the altar, to the preaching of the forgiveness of sins, to the glorious liberty of the sons of God.

> **So Eliphaz the Temanite and Bildad the Shuhite and Zophar the Naamathite went and did what the LORD had told them, and the LORD accepted Job's prayer.** (JOB 42:9)

You can almost imagine the Book of Second Job, where Satan appears before the Lord, who says, "Have you considered My servants Eliphaz, Bildad, and Zophar, that there are none like them on the earth, blameless and upright men who fear God and turn away from evil?" The heavenly conversation prevails. God's justifying of the sinner wins the day. The preaching of the altar will stand, and God's love and mercy stands against the demonic lie preached in suffering.

This same contest is played out in our lives when we suffer. The devil uses suffering to preach that God is angry, or that God is indifferent, or that God is not. He uses suffering to attack our faith, to tempt us to doubt God's mercy or despair of God's grace. The Lord doesn't refute this preaching. Instead, He lets the preaching of the altar and the preaching of the cross stand against it.

Our faith, after all, is not that the devil is wrong but that the Lord is right. The Gospel is true. Our sins are forgiven. God does love us.

The devil might use the evidence of our lives to convince us otherwise, but the cross stands as the unwavering evidence that Jesus is the Savior.

In the preaching of the cross, we see that God, in fact, does love us. He did not spare His own Son but gave Him up for us all (Romans 8:32). God gave His own Son because He loves the world (John 3:16). The light of the Gospel exposes how the devil lies through suffering.

15

Peter's Six Counsels to the Suffering

Be sober-minded; be watchful. Your adversary the devil prowls around like a roaring lion, seeking someone to devour. Resist him, firm in your faith, knowing that the same kinds of suffering are being experienced by your brotherhood throughout the world.

(1 PETER 5:8–9)

First Peter is a book about hope, and so it is a book about how to endure suffering. Six times in his five chapters, Peter takes up the topic of suffering and gives insight, wisdom, comfort, and hope to those who suffer (1 Peter 1:6–9; 2:20–24; 3:13–18a; 4:1–2; 4:12–19; 5:8–9).

We will consider these passages here.

FIRST COUNSEL: GOD USES SUFFERING TO REFINE OUR FAITH

In this you rejoice, though now for a little while, if necessary, you have been grieved by various trials, so that the

> **tested genuineness of your faith—more precious than gold that perishes though it is tested by fire—may be found to result in praise and glory and honor at the revelation of Jesus Christ. Though you have not seen Him, you love Him. Though you do not now see Him, you believe in Him and rejoice with joy that is inexpressible and filled with glory, obtaining the outcome of your faith, the salvation of your souls.** (1 PETER 1:6–9)

We rejoice in the hope of our salvation, the sure hope of the resurrection (1 Peter 1:3–5). Suffering comes to those who have this faith and joy in Christ, and it comes as a test.

We know that the devil uses suffering to try to destroy our faith. Peter tells us God's purpose in suffering: to test the genuineness of our faith.

Peter uses the picture of a metal refinery (see Malachi 3:2–3). Gold and silver are not entirely pure; other metals are always mixed in. Twenty-four-karat gold is almost 100 percent gold. Twelve-karat gold is 50 percent gold and 50 percent other metals. Sterling silver jewelry is often stamped with "925" because it is 92.5 percent silver. Fine silver is 99.9 percent silver. To purify these metals, you apply heat. When the metal is liquefied, the dross floats to the top. If the metal is pure, you see it when it's hot enough: there is no dross.

Peter says that our suffering is the fire that heats up our faith. If there is dross—disingenuousness, hypocrisy, and such—it is exposed. It floats to the surface, and, in suffering, the Lord takes these things away. "The crucible is for silver, and the furnace is for gold, and the LORD tests hearts" (Proverbs 17:3).

The devil uses suffering to attack and destroy our faith. The Lord Jesus uses suffering to strengthen and purify our faith. The result, Peter says, is that even though we don't see Jesus, we love Him, we believe in Him, we rejoice in His salvation, and this faith is more precious than any fine gold.

CHAPTER 15 | PETER'S SIX COUNSELS TO THE SUFFERING

SECOND COUNSEL: WE ARE CALLED TO SUFFERING

> For what credit is it if, when you sin and are beaten for it, you endure? But if when you do good and suffer for it you endure, this is a gracious thing in the sight of God. For to this you have been called, because Christ also suffered for you, leaving you an example, so that you might follow in His steps. He committed no sin, neither was deceit found in His mouth. When He was reviled, He did not revile in return; when He suffered, He did not threaten, but continued entrusting Himself to Him who judges justly. He Himself bore our sins in His body on the tree, that we might die to sin and live to righteousness. By His wounds you have been healed. (1 PETER 2:20–24)

The devil attacks our good works.

This is extremely frustrating. We expect that we will have trouble and grief because of our sins, because of the things we do wrong. But this would be helpful to us. If the devil attacked us when we did the wrong thing, we would think twice. Instead, he attacks our good works, he attacks our love, he causes us to suffer for doing good.

This, says Peter, is "a gracious thing in the sight of God."

We might be tempted to think that our suffering causes the Lord to despise us or to look away from us. "No," says Peter, "God delights in you still." And even more, Peter indicates that the Christian is called to a life of suffering. "To this [that is, to a life of suffering for doing good] you have been called!" Let that sink in.

The call to be a Christian is the call to suffer. The call to follow Jesus is the call to walk His way of suffering. If we are following Jesus, we are carrying a cross.

This text is the only place where Jesus is presented to us as an example. A generation ago, bracelets bearing the initials W.W.J.D.—"What would Jesus do?"—were a trend. We were supposed to ask this question and use it to guide our actions. Jesus was presented as the perfect example. This kind of thinking comes with problems. Namely, most of the things that Jesus did belong only to Him. He alone was born of a virgin. He alone is God in the flesh. He alone suffered God's wrath on the cross so that we would know God's love. When Jesus is acting as our Savior, He is not our example; He was in our place doing things for us. He was saving us because we cannot save ourselves.

Before He is our example, He is our Savior. But Peter does say that Jesus is our example, and in a very specific way. "For to this you have been called, because Christ also suffered for you, leaving you an example, so that you might follow in His steps."

There is a way, according to the prophets, that our worship conforms us to our gods. When the pagans worship gods made out of sticks, idols that cannot see or hear or speak, then the people become blind, deaf, and mute.

> Their idols are silver and gold,
>   the work of human hands.
> They have mouths, but do not speak;
>   eyes, but do not see.
> They have ears, but do not hear;
>   noses, but do not smell.
> They have hands, but do not feel;
>   feet, but do not walk;
>   and they do not make a sound in their throat.
> Those who make them become like them;
>   so do all who trust in them.
> (PSALM 115:4–8; SEE ALSO PSALM 135:16–18 AND ROMANS 1:21–24)

If this is true with the false gods which are no gods at all, then it is even more true with the true God. We are being "conformed to the image of His Son" (Romans 8:29). "And we all, with unveiled face, beholding the glory of the Lord, are being transformed into the same image from one degree of glory to another. For this comes from the Lord who is the Spirit" (2 Corinthians 3:18).

We are being conformed to Christ, to the one who suffered and died. His cross is stamped onto our lives. We follow His example. We suffer as Christ also suffered. If Peter has an answer to the problem of suffering, this is it: "Christ also suffered." And then Peter unfolds the glorious comfort of this suffering and death of God. "He Himself bore our sins in His body on the tree, that we might die to sin and live to righteousness. By His wounds you have been healed." Because we are healed by the wounds of Jesus, we can find comfort and even joy in our own wounds.

THIRD COUNSEL: A HEART PREPARED TO SUFFER

Now who is there to harm you if you are zealous for what is good? But even if you should suffer for righteousness' sake, you will be blessed. Have no fear of them, nor be troubled, but in your hearts honor Christ the Lord as holy, always being prepared to make a defense to anyone who asks you for a reason for the hope that is in you; yet do it with gentleness and respect, having a good conscience, so that, when you are slandered, those who revile your good behavior in Christ may be put to shame. For it is better to suffer for doing good, if that should be God's will, than for doing evil. For Christ also suffered once for sins, the righteous for the unrighteous, that He might bring us to God. (1 PETER 3:13–18A)

"Christ also suffered." We see it again. Christ the Righteous One suffered for the unrighteous to bring us to God. We have been brought to God. Our sins are forgiven. We are redeemed. We belong to the Lord. Peter gives us five things needed to be ready to suffer.

1. *Fearlessness.* "Have no fear of them . . ." "The LORD is on my side; I will not fear. What can man do to me?" (Psalm 118:6). Like death, pain and suffering are worshiped with fear, but

our fear belongs to God, and because our sins belong to Him as well, we have no fear.

2. *An untroubled heart.* ". . . nor be troubled . . ." Suffering wants to agitate us. But a calm and steady heart, anchored in Christ, is unmoved by the waves of trouble. Jesus gives us this command and comfort, "Let not your hearts be troubled. Believe in God; believe also in Me. . . . Peace I leave with you; My peace I give to you. Not as the world gives do I give to you. Let not your hearts be troubled, neither let them be afraid" (John 14:1, 27).

3. *Christ set apart in our heart.* ". . . but in your hearts honor Christ the Lord as holy . . . " It is Jesus we trust, Jesus we worship, Jesus we seek to serve. Jesus stands above our worries and our fears, our suffering and our distress. This is the key part of the text.

If it is our life, our comfort, or anything else that we have set apart in our hearts, that we consider to be holy and most important, then trouble will cause us to come unraveled. If we hold ourselves and our own good life to be most precious and dear to us, then trouble causes everything to crumble. If we have exalted our dreams of peace and comfort above all else, then suffering is devastating.

But if it is Jesus sitting there atop all the other things that we care about, then trouble, suffering, even persecution comes, astonishingly, as a blessing.

4. *Preparation to make a defense.* ". . . always being prepared to make a defense to anyone who asks you for a reason for the hope that is in you; yet do it with gentleness and respect . . ." Peter is specifically thinking of times of persecution, when the world brings trouble to the Christian because of their faith. Peter wants us to be ready to make the good confession.

In one way, this book is preparing you to do just that, to be ready to defend your hope. But in a most important and profound way, every

Christian already knows what they need to know. When you are asked what you believe, you confess: "I believe in God, the Father Almighty, Maker of heaven and earth. And in Jesus Christ, His only Son, our Lord, who was conceived by the Holy Spirit, born of the Virgin Mary, suffered under Pontius Pilate, was crucified, died, and was buried. He descended into hell. The third day He rose again from the dead. He ascended into heaven and sits at the right hand of God, the Father Almighty. From thence He will come to judge the living and the dead. I believe in the Holy Spirit, the holy Christian Church, the communion of saints, the forgiveness of sins, the resurrection of the body, and the life everlasting. Amen."

Or, if you don't have the time, you can simplify things: "Jesus is Lord. He is the Savior." Our study of the Scriptures and our Christian devotion is preparation for confession; we are being prepared to make a defense.

> 5. *A good conscience.* ". . . having a good conscience . . ." A conscience is made good before God by faith. Our conscience is clean when it knows that the blood of Jesus has washed and cleansed it from all sin.

A conscience is good before our neighbor by love. When we know we have acted as we ought, served and loved as we should, and asked for forgiveness where we have failed, then we have a good conscience with our neighbor. This kind of goodness is, in this life, always incomplete. We sin continually.

But we know the love of God in Christ. We know that God is not angry with us. We hear the voice of Jesus in our conscience, reassuring us of His redemption and grace. This gives us a readiness to suffer.

With a good conscience, we know that our suffering is not God's wrath over sin. He might, like a good father, be disciplining us and chastising us, but this is precisely because He loves us. (On this, see Hebrews 12:5–17.)

These five things—fearlessness, calm, Christ, preparation, and a good conscience—are the preparations of the heart for suffering. These are all gifts of the Gospel. With a heart thus prepared, we can receive suffering as a blessing. "But even if you should suffer for righteousness' sake, you will be blessed."

This is the teaching of Jesus.

> Blessed are those who are persecuted for righteousness' sake, for theirs is the kingdom of heaven. Blessed are you when others revile you and persecute you and utter all kinds of evil against you falsely on My account. Rejoice and be glad, for your reward is great in heaven, for so they persecuted the prophets who were before you. (MATTHEW 5:10–12)

Jesus doesn't say, "You'll make it through persecution. You'll endure trouble." He says that we are blessed when we are persecuted, blessed when we are reviled, blessed when the enemies of God speak evil against us. "Rejoice and be glad."

This is difficult but essential. Just as death wants to be worshiped by fear, so suffering wants to be worshiped by despair. The devil wants us to lose hope, wants to cause our faith to wither with suffering, but when we rejoice in our suffering, we refuse to let it be our god. We refuse to worship pain or pleasure.

This topic deserves further treatment. We'll take it up in the next section.

FOURTH COUNSEL: SUFFERING CURBS PASSIONS

> Since therefore Christ suffered in the flesh, arm yourselves with the same way of thinking, for whoever has suffered in the flesh has ceased from sin, so as to live for the rest of the time in the flesh no longer for human passions but for the will of God. (1 PETER 4:1–2)

When you are hurting, you are not lusting—that's the idea. The Lord uses our suffering to curb our appetites. Our flesh fights against the Spirit, and one of the ways our flesh is put to death is through suffering.

In part 4, we will take up the topic of our flesh, our sinful desires, and our passions—how the devil uses them to snuff out faith and what we should do about it. Here, we will simply note that the Christian can receive suffering as a gift. Even Jesus learned obedience through suffering (Hebrews 5:8), and the Lord has us in the same school.

St. Augustine had to wrestle with the question of Christian suffering: "If God loves you, why does He let you suffer along with the rest of the world?" Augustine answered with great Christian simplicity. God is doing one of two things with suffering: punishing sin or strengthening faith, and both are good for the Christian (*City of God*, Book 1, Chapter 9). Suffering does not hinder but rather helps the redeemed on their way to everlasting life.

FIFTH COUNSEL: SUFFERING IS NOT A SURPRISE

Beloved, do not be surprised at the fiery trial when it comes upon you to test you, as though something strange were happening to you. But rejoice insofar as you share Christ's sufferings, that you may also rejoice and be glad when His glory is revealed. If you are insulted for the name of Christ, you are blessed, because the Spirit of glory and of God rests upon you. But let none of you suffer as a murderer or a thief or an evildoer or as a meddler. Yet if anyone suffers as a Christian, let him not be ashamed, but let him glorify God in that name. For it is time for judgment to begin at the household of God; and if it begins with us, what will be the outcome for those who do not obey the gospel of God? And "If the righteous is scarcely saved, what will become of the ungodly and the sinner?" Therefore let those who suffer according to God's will entrust their souls to a faithful Creator while doing good. (1 PETER 4:12–19)

We are starting to see themes. Suffering tests us. Christ also suffered, so we share in His suffering. When we are insulted, we are blessed. We suffer not for evil deeds but for good works.

The key instruction in this passage is that we are to expect suffering. "Beloved, do not be surprised at the fiery trial when it comes upon you to test you, as though something strange were happening to you." Peter teaches us to expect suffering.

How much of the trouble in our lives comes from unmet expectations? We have the idea that our day is going to go this way, but instead it goes that way. We were hoping for a peaceful evening, instead we are visiting the urgent care center. We reach middle age and see what we had hoped for in life and what we have in life are totally different things. Unmet expectations are terrible.

Have you ever picked up a glass and taken a sip, expecting water but getting Sprite? Sprite tastes fine, but when you are expecting water, it's a shock, almost repulsive. That happens to me when I take a piece of candy, expecting something sweet, and get a mouth full of some sort of nasty licorice-salty thing. The taste is bad enough, but the shock of the unmet expectations makes it even worse. That's the power of unmet expectations, and that is what Peter is warning us about.

Don't expect an easy life. Don't expect boundless comfort. Don't expect that everyone will like you. Don't expect your faith to be respected or accepted. You live in a world that hates your Lord. You are going to have trouble. Don't be surprised.

This is really good advice, sound wisdom. When we run into trouble, especially when we run into persecution for being a Christian, we think, "What's going on here? I didn't sign up for this kind of trouble." We are shocked. "Surprised, are you?" says Peter as he hangs upside down on a cross.

Peter wants us to adjust our expectations. We should expect suffering.

> **I have said these things to you, that in Me you may have peace. In the world you will have tribulation. But take heart; I have overcome the world.** (JOHN 16:33)

> **[Paul and Barnabas were] strengthening the souls of the disciples, encouraging them to continue in the faith, and saying that through many tribulations we must enter the kingdom of God.** (ACTS 14:22)

[Let] no one be moved by these afflictions. For you yourselves know that we are destined for this. For when we were with you, we kept telling you beforehand that we were to suffer affliction, just as it has come to pass, and just as you know. (1 THESSALONIANS 3:3–4)

I have said all these things to you to keep you from falling away. They will put you out of the synagogues. Indeed, the hour is coming when whoever kills you will think he is offering service to God. And they will do these things because they have not known the Father, nor Me. But I have said these things to you, that when their hour comes you may remember that I told them to you. (JOHN 16:1–4)

Indeed, all who desire to live a godly life in Christ Jesus will be persecuted. (2 TIMOTHY 3:12)

We've been warned.

SIXTH COUNSEL: WE DO NOT SUFFER ALONE

Be sober-minded; be watchful. Your adversary the devil prowls around like a roaring lion, seeking someone to devour. Resist him, firm in your faith, knowing that the same kinds of suffering are being experienced by your brotherhood throughout the world. (1 PETER 5:8–9)

The devil likes us to think that we are alone in suffering, that we are the only ones who have tasted this bitter pill and felt this oppressing darkness. The devil always wants to add loneliness to our suffering. Peter knows better. Peter went from church to church, from country to country, and he saw how it was in the churches. He saw that the devil prowled around wherever the Word of God was preached. He saw that trouble and persecution was the universal experience of the Christian.

"You are not alone," Peter reminds us, and it is a good and comforting reminder. Your fellow Christians are also suffering. And, don't forget, your Lord Himself suffered, suffered to rescue us from the devil.

The devil attacks through suffering, but the Lord blesses through suffering, and we delight in His blessings. We know that suffering strengthens our faith, weakens our sinful flesh, marks us as Christians, binds us together, teaches us to trust and to serve and to wait on the Lord, who is bringing us through this life to the glory of the resurrection.

16

Joy in Suffering

Count it all joy, my brothers, when
you meet trials of various kinds.

(JAMES 1:2)

The Bible teaches us that we should rejoice in suffering. This does not mean that we like suffering, that we enjoy painful stuff. If we liked it, then it wouldn't be suffering.

We recognize that suffering is the result of the fall. Jesus delivers us "out of the great tribulation" (Revelation 7:14). He delivers us from evil. We were never meant to suffer, and the day is coming soon when every tear will be wiped from our eyes (Revelation 7:17), and there will be no more suffering.

But as Jesus has taken up the tool of suffering to redeem us from sin, death, and the devil, so He sanctifies suffering for us and uses suffering to sanctify us. The Scriptures tell us of a joy that lives through suffering, that endures suffering. And even something more. When we know the source and the purpose God intends in suffering, this knowledge lets us receive suffering as a gift.

We'll consider the Scriptures on the topic of joy in suffering.

First, we'll return to the Sermon on the Mount. Jesus begins His sermon on the kingdom of God talking about blessings. In the Lord's kingdom, things work differently. The kingdom of heaven belongs to the poor in spirit. The meek inherit the earth. There is blessing in persecution.

> Blessed are those who are persecuted for righteousness' sake, for theirs is the kingdom of heaven. Blessed are you when others revile you and persecute you and utter all kinds of evil against you falsely on My account. Rejoice and be glad, for your reward is great in heaven, for so they persecuted the prophets who were before you. (MATTHEW 5:10–12)

Persecution numbers us with the prophets! Persecution from the world means that we are not a part of that kingdom! Persecution is a mark of the Church, and when we see and feel this persecution, we rejoice that we are part of the Lord's persecuted kingdom, His eternal reign.

Jesus preaches a similar sermon, using even more intense language, which Luke records.

> Blessed are you when people hate you and when they exclude you and revile you and spurn your name as evil, on account of the Son of Man! Rejoice in that day, and leap for joy, for behold, your reward is great in heaven; for so their fathers did to the prophets. (LUKE 6:22–23)

Leap for joy! Jump up and down! This is how we should react when we are persecuted! Imagine it.

This is how it was in the Book of Acts. The apostles were brought before the Sanhedrin, forbidden to preach the name of Jesus, and beaten. The text tells us, "Then they left the presence of the council, rejoicing that they were counted worthy to suffer dishonor for the name" (Acts 5:41).

Why does Jesus say that we should leap up and down with joy and rejoicing over persecution? "Your reward in great in heaven." We are not laboring for an earthly reward or an earthly kingdom. It would do us no good to gain the entire world and lose our soul (Matthew 16:26). We are storing up our treasure in heaven (Matthew 6:19–21).

When Jesus says to the persecuted that their reward is great in heaven, He is not indicating that our suffering earns salvation. Only the blood of Jesus takes away sins. We are saved by His grace through faith, not our own works and efforts. Jesus is reminding us that we are citizens of another kingdom, that our joys are in another place, our treasures are not here.

And more—our heroes are the prophets who treasured God's Word, believed God's promises, and preached the Law and the Gospel. These heroes of ours were also persecuted for the Lord's name. When our names are put on the list of the persecuted, we are on the list with the prophets! This gives us great joy.

Paul picks up the theme of joy in suffering, something he learned through experience. Paul's work was marked with one trouble after another. He was beaten, whipped, stoned, lowered out of windows, shipwrecked, jailed, rejected, insulted, abused, slandered, abandoned, sent out of town in the middle of the night. He spent most of his last years in prison, and he was near death countless times. (Paul outlines all his troubles in 2 Corinthians 11:23–33.)

Still he says, "I have learned in whatever situation I am to be content. I know how to be brought low, and I know how to abound. In any and every circumstance, I have learned the secret of facing plenty and hunger, abundance and need" (Philippians 4:11–12).

Paul is content, even in trouble. "For the sake of Christ, then, I am content with weaknesses, insults, hardships, persecutions, and calamities. For when I am weak, then I am strong" (2 Corinthians 12:10).

And Paul is more than content. He has joy in the midst of sorrow. "Rejoice in the Lord always; again I will say, rejoice" (Philippians 4:4). Specifically, Paul gives these instructions about joy in suffering:

> **Not only that, but we rejoice in our sufferings, knowing that suffering produces endurance, and endurance produces character, and character produces hope, and hope does not put us to shame, because God's love has been poured into our hearts through the Holy Spirit who has been given to us.** (Romans 5:3–5)

This is an incredible passage, overflowing with wisdom.

We know that the devil, through our suffering, attacks our faith. He wants us to doubt the promises God has given us in Christ. The devil also, in our suffering, attacks our hope, that is, our faith in the promises of God not yet fulfilled. We hope for the Last Day. We hope for the resurrection of the body. We hope for the new heaven and new earth, where righteousness will dwell. We hope for the deliverance from this life of trouble. This Christian hope has no uncertainty. (Our normal use of hope is full of uncertainty. "I hope it will rain this week." "I hope I'll get an A on that test." We hope, but we are not sure.) Christian hope is sure. It is sure because God cannot lie. It is sure because His promises are sure. Christian hope is simply faith directed to the future.

The devil uses suffering to attack our hope. He wants us to think, "Today is bad; tomorrow will be the same. Or worse." The devil wants to snuff out the light at the end of the tunnel, the thought of the dawn, our longing for what is to come.

We are attacked by hopelessness.

The Lord, with a kind of spiritual jujitsu, always turns the devil's attack back onto himself. The devil drove Jesus to the cross. The Lord triumphed over the devil on the cross. The devil attacks the Word. The Lord sends the devil away with His Word. The devil attacks faith through suffering. The Lord uses our suffering to test and strengthen our faith. And now we see that the devil uses suffering to attack hope, and the Lord turns it around. He uses suffering to build us up in hope. (The same thing is true with joy and love. The devil uses sorrow to attack joy and love, and the Lord uses the same to strengthen the same.)

Paul connects the dots from suffering to hope: "Suffering produces endurance, and endurance produces character, and character produces hope."

But we do not only rejoice in suffering because it produces hope but also because we *know* it produces hope. "We rejoice in our sufferings, *knowing* that suffering produces endurance," and so on. We rejoice because we know, we understand what the devil is doing with suffering, and we understand the Lord's counterattack. We know that there are things that the Lord wants to give us—things such as endurance and character—and the only way to get them is in the school of suffering. James continues this theme as he begins his letter.

> **Count it all joy, my brothers, when you meet trials of various kinds, for you know that the testing of your faith produces steadfastness.** (JAMES 1:2–3)

Trials test your faith. Testing makes steadfastness. You know it.

I heard a story about the Biosphere 2, a huge terrarium built in the desert in Arizona, designed to be a self-contained ecosystem with a farm, a rain forest, a desert, and other environmental zones. There was trouble with the trees. They didn't grow properly because there was no wind. For the wood in the trunk to harden and hold the weight of the branches, the tree needs to be bent and buffeted by the wind. There are benefits to suffering. This is part of our basic human wisdom, and the Scriptures explain why. Suffering produces endurance, endurance produces character, and character lives in hope. The Lord sturdies us up in suffering.

We've heard from Jesus, from Paul, and from James. Let's add one more voice to the mix: St. Peter. This verse is part of Peter's fifth counsel on suffering.

> **But rejoice insofar as you share Christ's sufferings, that you may also rejoice and be glad when His glory is revealed.** (1 PETER 4:13)

Our suffering is not disconnected from the suffering of Jesus but bound up with it. Jesus suffered for us to win our salvation. Jesus now suffers alongside His Church, in His Christians. We suffer with Christ and for the name of Christ. We are despised, persecuted, rejected, scorned, mocked, and ridiculed. Just like Jesus.

When we are despised and hated by the world, not only are we numbered with the prophets and apostles, the saints and martyrs, but we are also numbered with Christ. The suffering of the Christian is directly bound up with the suffering of Jesus. We share the same enemies as our

Lord, and just as the world hated Jesus, so it hates us. This is our joy, even our boast.

This joy is our protection.

Consider the spiritual dynamics of this joy in suffering. The devil, through suffering, wants to wreck our faith, diminish our love, steal our hope, murder our joy. Jesus won't have it. He gives us joy in the midst of suffering, and this joy of the Lord is our strength (Nehemiah 8:10). As we rejoice in our troubles and tribulation, we take away the devil's motivation to cause us to suffer. As we rejoice in our suffering, we use the devil's attacks against him. When we leap for joy when we are rejected by the world, we shove the devil's nose in the victory of the cross.

Remember from the parable of the sower the seed that landed in the rocks. The problem was not the sun but the roots. The problem is not our suffering. The trouble is not the scorching heat of this life. If our roots are sunk deep into the Lord's Word, the sun of suffering comes to us as a blessing and a gift.

Paul reminds us, "It has been granted to you that for the sake of Christ you should not only believe in Him but also suffer for His sake" (Philippians 1:29).

God be praised for His gift of suffering.

> So we do not lose heart. Though our outer self is wasting away, our inner self is being renewed day by day. For this light momentary affliction is preparing for us an eternal weight of glory beyond all comparison, as we look not to the things that are seen but to the things that are unseen. For the things that are seen are transient, but the things that are unseen are eternal. (2 CORINTHIANS 4:16–18)

IN
THE
WEEDS

Public Domain/The MET Museum

ROMANUS: MARTYR. HERO.
AD 303. ANTIOCH.

The Christians in Antioch were being persecuted. Romanus, a deacon in Caesarea, traveled up to Antioch to strengthen the Christians. "The wolves are attacking the flock, but don't be afraid." The Lord used this preaching of Romanus to strengthen the faith of the Christians, and all of them—old men and women, fathers and mothers, young children—were ready to be martyred. None would renounce their faith and offer the sacrifice to Caesar. Instead, they all stuck out their necks for the sword, ready to die for their faith.

Asclepiades was the captain in charge of the persecution. He asked who was the cause of this rebellion, and learning of Romanus, he had him bound and brought before him. "Are you the cause of this sedition? Are you going to be the cause of so much death? You will suffer in the same way that you have caused others to suffer."

Romanus was not afraid. Quite the opposite. "I joyfully accept your sentence," he answered the captain. "I'm ready to be sacrificed for my brethren."

The captain was enraged. "Tie him up. Tear him open. Pour out his bowels." The soldiers protested. "It is not right to do that to a nobleman." "Then scourge him with whips with the lead tips." Instead of tears or groans, Romanus sang psalms as he was whipped and told the soldiers not to favor him because of his nobility. "It's not my family, it's my Christian faith that makes me noble."

Romanus preached through the torture, mocking the pagan gods, warning the captain that he would be judged by the Creator of heaven and earth. The captain had his sides lanced so that his ribs were exposed, and Romanus said, "I'm sorry, not at my injuries, but that you believe lies."

Romanus preached Christ. He urged the captain and all who could hear him to turn from their idolatry and trust in the blood of Jesus for eternal life. Asclepiades commanded Romanus to be struck in the mouth to stop his preaching. They knocked out all his teeth. They tore his eyelids with their nails. They cut open his cheeks with knives. They pulled out his beard with chunks of flesh.

To this Romanus said, "I thank thee, O captain, that thou hast opened unto me many mouths, whereby I may preach my Lord and Savior Christ. Look how many wounds I have, so many mouths I have, lauding and praising God."

Romanus: Martyr. Hero.

We'll meet in the resurrection.

17

In the Weeds: The Lust of the Flesh and the Pride of Life

---

*As for what was sown among thorns, this is
the one who hears the word, but the cares
of the world and the deceitfulness of riches
choke the word, and it proves unfruitful.*

(MATTHEW 13:22)

The third attack on the seed of the Word is the weeds and the thorns. This seed reached the ground and grew, but other plants grew up around them and cut them off from the sun. They were choked out and died. Jesus explains what the weeds are: "the cares of the world, the deceitfulness of riches." These are the temptations of the sinful flesh, the false desires that drive us to sin.

Jesus is here warning us about the dangers of pleasure. This is the opposite of the seed that falls among the rocks. There the devil attacked us with pain and sorrow. Here the devil attacks us with pleasure and delight, with indulgence. He hands us over to the bad things that we want; he will give us the world if it will cause us to lose our soul (Matthew 16:26).

Suffering was an attack from the outside. Pleasure is an attack from the inside.

Suffering wants to be worshiped by fear. The things of this world want to be worshiped with love, desire, lust. John warns us about this love.

> **Do not love the world or the things in the world. If anyone loves the world, the love of the Father is not in him. For all that is in the world—the desires of the flesh and the desires of the eyes and pride of life—is not from the Father but is from the world. And the world is passing away along with its desires, but whoever does the will of God abides forever.** (1 JOHN 2:15–17)

When we pursue the things of this world, we are chasing after death. A part of us longs for this death—the corrupt sinful nature that wants always the wrong thing. The Bible calls this "the flesh." (The word *flesh* does not always refer to our sinful nature. It sometimes refers to our physicality and other times to our ancestry. The context will always make this clear.) It is the third great enemy of God's Word.

There is, inside of us, a traitor, a saboteur, a demonic ally that pushes us to sin, that fights against God and His kingdom.

18

Our Sinful Flesh

As was the man of dust, so also are those
who are of the dust, and as is the man of heaven,
so also are those who are of heaven. Just as we
have borne the image of the man of dust, we
shall also bear the image of the man of heaven.
(1 CORINTHIANS 15:48–49)

Let's talk about our sinful flesh. We want to understand our fallen nature, especially to understand how the devil uses it to tempt us to sin.

It starts in the Garden of Eden. The fall into sin wrecked everything.

There was no death before the fall. Now everything is dying.

There was no corruption. Now everything is falling apart.

There was no temptation. Now sin crouches at the door, waiting to devour us.

There was no sin. Now all have sinned and fallen short of the glory of God.

We were created in the image and likeness of God. We now bear the image of Adam, the man of dust.

We had the knowledge of good. Now we have the knowledge of good and evil.

We were created as the friends of God. Now we are His enemies.

We were created to be the children of God. Now we are children of wrath.

There was no wrath of God, no heavenly anger. Now there is the very clear and present danger of eternal condemnation.

The fall wrecked everything.

One of the most horrifying results of this corruption of our nature is that we don't know how bad we really are. We don't feel the pain of our utter sinfulness.

The Church Fathers would often use the example of leprosy, a terrible skin disease that rots away the flesh. One of the symptoms of leprosy is the loss of feeling. The disease damages the nerve endings so that you can't feel pain. If you had leprosy on your foot and stubbed your toe, you wouldn't know it. If you had leprosy on your hand and broke your finger, you wouldn't know. In a similar way, we are so profoundly sinful we don't even know it or feel it. We must be told in the Scriptures.

So we want to consider the Scriptures to understand our sinful condition. Here are five consequences of the fall as it relates to our sinful flesh.

1. WE BECAME GUILTY.

We broke God's Law. We transgressed His singular prohibition. "Have you eaten of the tree of which I commanded you not to eat?" (Genesis 3:11). Adam and Eve were guilty, sentenced to death. God expelled them from the garden, handed them over to difficulty. We've inherited this difficulty, and we've inherited this death. "Therefore, just as sin came into the world through one man, and death through sin, and so death spread to all men because all sinned" (Romans 5:12).

All mankind fell through Adam's fall. "Because of one man's trespass, death reigned through that one man" (Romans 5:17). All are guilty before God, all fall short of His glory.

2. WE LOST THE IMAGE OF GOD.

When we were created in God's image, we had an original righteousness. We believed and loved God above all things. We worshiped God alone. We had an innate desire to do good. That was lost.

God created Adam and Eve in His own image and likeness, but listen to how Moses describes the birth of Seth:

> When God created man, He made him in the likeness of God. Male and female He created them, and He blessed them and named them Man when they were created. When Adam had lived 130 years, he fathered a son in his own likeness, after his image, and named him Seth. (GENESIS 5:1–3)

Adam bore the image of God. Seth bore the image of Adam.

> As was the man of dust, so also are those who are of the dust, and as is the man of heaven, so also are those who are of heaven. Just as we have borne the image of the man of dust, we shall also bear the image of the man of heaven. (1 CORINTHIANS 15:48–49)

No righteousness. No perfection. No eternal life.

But the loss of the image of God is not only a lack. Into the vacuum comes a corruption, an evil, a sinful nature.

3. OUR HUMAN NATURE WAS CORRUPTED AND BECOME UTTERLY SINFUL.

In place of original righteousness, we now have original sin, a thorough corruption of our human nature, which we've inherited from Adam. We are "brought forth in iniquity," sinful even from the moment of conception (Psalm 51:5).

This means that we are sinners and guilty before God, even if we never committed an actual sin. We are sinners by nature.

Here's how the old Lutheran forefathers talked about this inner corruption:

> Original sin (in human nature) is not just this entire absence of all good in spiritual, divine things. Original sin is more than the lost image of God in mankind; it is at the same time also a deep, wicked, horrible, fathomless, mysterious, and unspeakable corruption of the entire human

145

nature and all its powers. It is especially a corruption of the soul's highest, chief powers in the understanding, heart, and will. So now, since the fall, a person inherits an inborn wicked disposition and inward impurity of heart, an evil lust and tendency. We all by disposition and nature inherit from Adam a heart, feeling, and thought that are, according to their highest powers and the light of reason, naturally inclined and disposed directly against God and His chief commandments. Yes, they are hostile toward God, especially in divine and spiritual things. For in other respects, regarding natural, outward things that are subject to reason, a person still has power, ability, and to a certain degree understanding—although very much weakened. All of this, however, has been so infected and contaminated by original sin that it is of no use before God. (Formula of Concord, Solid Declaration I 11–12)

That is strong language—"deep, wicked, horrible, fathomless, mysterious, and unspeakable corruption of the entire human nature and all its powers"! That is our sinful flesh.

When we were originally created in God's image we naturally wanted the right things. That has changed. We now want the wrong stuff. Our flesh has crooked desires and corrupt passions.

> For the desires of the flesh are against the Spirit, and the desires of the Spirit are against the flesh, for these are opposed to each other, to keep you from doing the things you want to do. (Galatians 5:17)

> But put on the Lord Jesus Christ, and make no provision for the flesh, to gratify its desires. (Romans 13:14)

> Beloved, I urge you as sojourners and exiles to abstain from the passions of the flesh, which wage war against your soul. (1 Peter 2:11)

. . . among whom we all once lived in the passions of
our flesh, carrying out the desires of the body and the
mind, and were by nature children of wrath, like the rest
of mankind. (Ephesians 2:3)

This corruption of our desires has a theological name: concupiscence.
We are bent away from God toward sin and every evil. We are inclined
always toward sin. (Remember, we are here talking about the natural
man apart from the work of the Spirit of God.)
What are these sinful desires?

For out of the heart come evil thoughts, murder, adultery, sexual immorality, theft, false witness, slander.
(Matthew 15:19)

Now the works of the flesh are evident: sexual immorality, impurity, sensuality, idolatry, sorcery, enmity, strife,
jealousy, fits of anger, rivalries, dissensions, divisions, envy,
drunkenness, orgies, and things like these. (Galatians 5:19–21)

If there is a commandment from God, our sinful flesh wants to break it.
We are not spiritually neutral. We are born as God's enemies, and
our sinful flesh actively fights against God.

4. The punishment for our sin is death, eternal condemnation, and other miseries in this life.

God is not indifferent about our sinful condition. St. Paul warns
us: "Put to death therefore what is earthly in you: sexual immorality,
impurity, passion, evil desire, and covetousness, which is idolatry. On
account of these the wrath of God is coming" (Colossians 3:5–6).

Our sinful flesh sets us as the enemies of God and the rightful object
of His anger: "For the wrath of God is revealed from heaven against all
ungodliness and unrighteousness of men" (Romans 1:18).

5. ONLY JESUS CAN RESCUE US FROM OUR SINFUL CORRUPTION.

The depth of our sin and the corruption of our nature mean, among other things, that we cannot save ourselves. We do not have the strength or the resources to attain righteousness or life. Our condition is so desperate that we need a Savior. We have one in Christ.

Jesus saves us from our sin, from death, from the wrath of God. He delivers us. And He begins to work in us to rescue us from our own flesh. This work is only begun in this life and won't be completed until the resurrection of the dead. But it is begun, and the Lord continues to fight with and for us.

19

Lust Lives in Every Commandment

*What causes quarrels and what causes
fights among you? Is it not this, that your
passions are at war within you? You desire
and do not have, so you murder. You covet
and cannot obtain, so you fight and quarrel.*

(JAMES 4:1–2)

We will consider our flesh, what it wants, how the devil uses it, and how the Lord sets us to fight against it.

What is it that our sinful flesh wants? Our desires take all kinds of shapes. Some are easier to recognize than others. The devil loves to work in darkness, and it is no different when he teams up with our flesh. He wants to hide and confuse our own disordered desires.

We can use the order God has put in place to see what the fall has put out of order. Right desires are ordered according to the Ten Commandments. We can use the Ten Commandments, then, to recognize the different shapes and sizes of our sinful desires.

We'll start with the Second Table of the Law, the last seven commandments, which deal with our love for our neighbor.

The Fourth Commandment says, "Honor your father and your mother." Our sinful flesh is rebellious and wants no authority to be placed over us.

The Fifth Commandment says, "You shall not murder." Our flesh is angry, especially toward our enemies, and indifferent toward others' needs.

The Sixth Commandment says, "You shall not commit adultery." Our flesh is lustful, wanting sexual pleasure in all sorts of wrong ways.

The Seventh Commandment says, "You shall not steal." Our sinful flesh is greedy and lazy. We want more, and we think that there is security and happiness in that more.

The Eighth Commandment says, "You shall not give false testimony against your neighbor." Our flesh is bitter and proud. We want our own name and reputation to stand above all else.

The Ninth and Tenth Commandments forbid us from coveting, but that is the very nature and essence of our flesh's problem. We want the stuff that we shouldn't want. We don't want the stuff that we should. Eve saw the fruit, that it was good for food, and she reached out and took it. Covetousness is at the root of the problem.

When it comes to the first three commandments, our sinful flesh will fear, love, and trust just about anything but God. We replace the true God with various idols, the Sixth Commandment idols of pleasure, the Seventh Commandment idol of mammon, or any of the thousand other false gods that we crafted in order to have religion without repentance.

Our flesh refuses to be bound by the Ten Commandments—in its actions, in its desires, and even in its understanding of what is good.

We'll consider, in the next chapters, how the devil uses the desires of our flesh to lie about freedom. It is worth noting here how the devil lies about what is good and holy. We see it most especially in our culture's conversation about love.

The devil has a vested interest in abstracting and redefining love. If he can convince us that love is a feeling, found in ourselves, then he can disconnect love from the commandments of God. He can use love against the commandments of God. This, in fact, is what has happened.

It is easiest to see with the Sixth Commandment and the devil's assault on marriage.

The argument that two men or two women can be married passed through the Supreme Court a few years back. It was an argument from abstract love, that you can't stop two people from loving each other. "Love wins" was on the celebratory rainbow flags outside the court. This is not a new argument. For years, the young men have said to the young ladies, "If we love each other, how can it be wrong?" Sexual immorality, which is wrong, is made "right" by the claim of love.

Jesus taught that love is a summary of the Law. When asked what the greatest commandment was, He responded,

> The most important is, "Hear, O Israel: The Lord our God, the Lord is one. And you shall love the Lord your God with all your heart and with all your soul and with all your mind and with all your strength." The second is this: "You shall love your neighbor as yourself." There is no other commandment greater than these. (MARK 12:29–31)

If you boil down the commandments to their essence, you find love.

> Owe no one anything, except to love each other, for the one who loves another has fulfilled the law. For the commandments, "You shall not commit adultery, You shall not murder, You shall not steal, You shall not covet," and any other commandment, are summed up in this word: "You shall love your neighbor as yourself." Love does no wrong to a neighbor; therefore love is the fulfilling of the law. (ROMANS 13:8–10)

How is it, then, that love is set against the commandments? That love is used as reason and motivation to break the commandments? And, this last trick is amazing, that love is used against Christians, who are called haters?

"Who are you to judge my love?"

The answer to this question (which generally isn't actually looking for an answer) is this: I'm a human being. It is our job to judge our loves, to assess our affections, to discern the helpfulness and rightness of our desires.

Let's pretend, for a moment, that there was a man who loved licking the tires on strangers' cars. "I love it," he says. "It makes me happy. No one gets hurt. Who are you to judge me? How can you tell me that what I love is bad or wrong?" If love, defined as a strong desire to do what makes me happy, stands above all else, then there is no way of saying to this poor fellow, "You shouldn't lick those tires." We know this is wrong. Our desires are subject to something more, to right and wrong. Love should not be set against the commandments of God. The Ten Commandments are God's definition of love.

Love takes shape according to the Ten Commandments and according to our vocations in the three estates. We often hear talk of "true love." I think we need to talk about "truthed" love—love that has been checked against the square of reason and God's Law.

I have a terrible eye for the square. If I hang a picture or a shelf without a level, it is notoriously crooked. Keri will say, "Why did you make that picture slanted?" I need a level to make sure it is square. The Ten Commandments are like a level for our love. "Is this love?" "No," the Ten Commandments say, "that is lust." "What about this?" "Nope, that's greed." "What about this?" "Yes, that is charity."

The Ten Commandments let us know if our passions are good or bad, if our thoughts are good or bad, if our aims and goals are good or bad, and thus they encourage or discourage our wants and desires. The Ten Commandments help discern if we are driven by our love for ourselves or by our love for God and our neighbor. The Ten Commandments are the rule to determine if the things we want are good or not. They bridle the passions.

Love set against the commandments is not love. It might feel like love, but that is a lie. And love is only one example.

Our sinful flesh is always looking for noble motivations to break the commandments. We use "justice" to defend our anger. We use "compassion" to justify our theft. We use "responsibility" to cover our greed. We use "prayer lists" to conceal our gossip. Pick your vice; we've got a virtue to hide it.

Our sinful flesh is passionate in its rebellion against God and His ordering of the world. Our flesh is busy tearing against the commandments. It wants the opposite of what God intends.

We shouldn't leave this subject without a quick mention of vocation. Just like the Ten Commandments, our vocation or station also gives shape to our love. Or, to say that a different way, love is shaped by our callings. People have often noted that the Greeks were onto this idea. They had lots of different words for love. *Eros* is sexual love; *phileo* is brotherly love; *storge* is familial love; *agape* is selfless, sacrificial, unconditional love and is often used to describe that love Jesus has for us. This is a good start, but we can go further.

There is a Fourth Commandment love in the family, with a different shape to that love depending on if you are the parent or the child. The love of a child for a parent looks different than the love of a parent for a child. The parent's love sounds like "It's bedtime," and the child's love sounds like "Okay." If the kids are telling their parents to go to bed, then things are out of order. The shape and look of that love changes as the children get older. "Honor your father and mother" looks very different when you are an adult; your love takes a different shape.

There is a Sixth Commandment love of husband and wife that is very unique and exclusive. It includes sexual intimacy, but much more. This love belongs uniquely to marriage.

There is a Fifth Commandment love for life that sets up to bless and protect our neighbor. This looks different if you are a soldier than if you are a doctor.

There is a Seventh Commandment love that looks like generosity. This looks different if you are a boss than if you are a worker.

There is a Third Commandment love, which is a delight in the Lord's Word and going to church. This looks different for the pastor than for the parishioner. My love for the members of Hope Lutheran Church looks like me preaching and teaching and praying. Their love for me is listening, discerning, believing the Lord's Word.

A final note on this: with this understanding of the different shapes of love, we can give a fuller response to the challenge we talked about earlier. When the argument comes to us, say, from two men who would like to be married, "Who are you to say that we can't love each other?" we respond, "You should love each other. In fact, you are commanded in the Bible to love one another. But your love for each another is different than the love of a husband and a wife. Your love should not take shape according to the Sixth Commandment. The love you are after is what we call friendship."

Love is not the problem—rather, love rightly understood. The devil wants to hide our sinful desires behind love, but the Ten Commandments put things in order. We have a *truthed* love. While the devil wants us to live toward the sinful desires of our flesh, the Lord sends us to our neighbor and to God with a rightly ordered love.

> **But each person is tempted when he is lured and enticed by his own desire. Then desire when it has conceived gives birth to sin, and sin when it is fully grown brings forth death.** (JAMES 1:14–15)

20

The Anatomy of Temptation

The devil finds a friend in our sinful flesh.

It is horrifying to remember how God found Adam and Eve in the garden, wrapped in fig leaves, hiding *with the devil*. The devil presents himself to us as our friend, and he uses our flesh to do it.

We saw how it worked with Adam and Eve. He didn't stuff the forbidden fruit down their throats. He came alongside them and enticed them. The fruit is not bad. "You will not surely die" (Genesis 3:4). The fruit is good. "When you eat of it your eyes will be opened, and you will be like God" (Genesis 3:5). And, finally, the devil makes God the bad guy, the liar. "Did God actually say? . . . God knows . . ." (Genesis 3:1, 5).

> So when the woman saw that the tree was good for food, and that it was a delight to the eyes, and that the tree was to be desired to make one wise, she took of its fruit and ate, and she also gave some to her husband who was with her, and he ate. (GENESIS 3:6)

They ate of their own free will. False desire leads to sin which leads to death. This is the anatomy of temptation.

> But each person is tempted when he is lured and enticed by his own desire. Then desire when it has conceived gives

> **birth to sin, and sin when it is fully grown brings forth death.** (JAMES 1:14–15)

If it worked on Adam and Eve, humanity in its glory, imagine how it works on us. The devil works on our desires, he stokes the flames of our sinful passions, and we take it from there. We do the sinning, and we do the dying, because we want to!

Temptation, then, is an attack on our wanting and an assault on our desires. The devil spurs on our own flesh to lie to us, and in the process, he makes God into the bad guy. If we could hear the conversation between the devil and our sinful flesh, it would sound something like this:

Devil: *"Hey, friend, good to see you."*

Our Flesh: *"Oh, hey."*

Devil: *"So, you want to do that thing?"*

Our Flesh: *"I sure do. Wow, you really get me."*

Devil: *"You know it. And you know what else? I want you to do that thing too! I'm on your team. But, if you don't mind me asking, what's stopping you?"*

Our Flesh: *"God. He's got these commandments . . ."*

Devil: *"Ah, I've heard of that guy. He's no fun. He's always stopping people from doing what they want to do."*

Our Flesh: *"Tell me about it."*

Devil: *"God wants people to live how He wants them to live and not how they want to live. He wants you to be His slave. I think you should be free, free to do what you want to do. It's good to be free."*

Our Flesh: *"That is exactly what I wanted to hear."*

We'll notice three things about this conversation.

First, the devil has material to work with. We already want to sin. We want to do wrong stuff. We have sinful desires. Second, the devil uses those desires to position himself as our friend and God as our enemy. Third, the devil uses our sinful desires to redefine freedom. Doing what we want, chasing our desires, living for our pleasures—this is freedom. Keeping God's commandments, the devil wants us to believe, is bondage. This is a lie, but a lie we love to hear.

I'm convinced, in my short life of observing things in the church, that this is the reason that most people leave the church and lose their faith. There are things that they want to do, some sin that they want to commit, and the Word of God gets in the way, so they throw it out. It doesn't happen instantly. The thorns and the weeds take a while to grow, but eventually the light of God's Word is choked out, and faith dies. Everything dies.

> **For when you were slaves of sin, you were free in regard to righteousness. But what fruit were you getting at that time from the things of which you are now ashamed? For the end of those things is death.** (Romans 6:20–21)

The things of this world are fading away, and when we love them, worship them, desire them and chase after these desires, then we chain ourselves to a sinking ship.

> **Their end is destruction, their god is their belly, and they glory in their shame, with minds set on earthly things.** (Philippians 3:19)

> **The world is passing away along with its desires.** (1 John 2:17)

> **For while we were living in the flesh, our sinful passions, aroused by the law, were at work in our members to bear fruit for death.** (Romans 7:5)

The devil, under the guise of friendship, wants to lash us to sin. The devil, disguised as a helper, wants to chain us to death. The devil, pretending to emancipate us, leads us with him into prison.

157

Jesus says with truth and clarity, "Truly, truly, I say to you, everyone who practices sin is a slave to sin" (John 8:34). And then, for us, "If the Son sets you free, you will be free indeed" (John 8:36). Jesus sets us free from sin, from death, and He has begun the work of freeing us from our passions, from the coercive control of sinful desires.

21

Sex and Money

Let marriage be held in honor among all,
and let the marriage bed be undefiled, for God
will judge the sexually immoral and adulterous.
Keep your life free from love of money, and
be content with what you have, for He has said,
"I will never leave you nor forsake you."

(HEBREWS 13:4–5)

As the Scriptures warn us about the dangers of the flesh, two commandments come to the top again and again: six and seven. "You shall not commit adultery." "You shall not steal." Sex and money. Paul warns the Ephesians about these twin dangers.

> For you may be sure of this, that everyone who is sexually immoral or impure, or who is covetous (that is, an idolater), has no inheritance in the kingdom of Christ and God. Let no one deceive you with empty words, for because of these things the wrath of God comes upon the sons of disobedience. Therefore do not become partners with them; for at one time you were darkness, but now you are light in the Lord. Walk as children of light. (EPHESIANS 5:5–8)

To return to the parable of the sower, these two temptations seem to be the most pervasive weeds in the field. Add fame to the mix and we have a fleshly canopy that threatens to strangle the faith.

Because of the threat, and because of the broad array of Scriptures devoted to these two topics, we will give them each consideration.

In Pursuit of Chastity

Let marriage be held in honor among all, and let the marriage bed be undefiled. (Hebrews 13:4)

The Christian sexual ethic is straightforward: the act of sex is reserved for marriage. There is a bit more to it, but this is a good starting point. Sex is to be protected by the bonds of holy matrimony.

This means, first, that the Scriptures do not treat sex as bad. God gave the commandment and blessing to Adam and Eve: "Be fruitful and multiply" (Genesis 1:28) and "They shall become one flesh" (Genesis 2:24). What we today call a sex drive began with those words of God. Martin Luther understood it this way: "For the Word of God which created you and said, 'Be fruitful and multiply,' abides and rules within you; you can by no means ignore it, or you will be bound to commit heinous sins without end" (AE 45:19).

Not only can sex be a good work, but sexual desire is something like a law of nature and, when it is rightly ordered in marriage, is also a blessing. We know that the act of marriage is much more than physical pleasure. From sex comes the great blessing of children. The Lord designed intimacy to bind husband and wife together, to form and strengthen their union.

Christians often talk about abstinence. I think it is much better to speak of chastity. First, abstinence is a purely negative term—"don't do this." It speaks only of avoidance, not of pursuit. It is true that the unmarried are to be abstinent, but that only tells them what not to do. Chastity includes abstinence but is more. Chastity is positive; it means living in support of sexual purity. We can say to the unmarried "pursue chastity." This is something that requires courage and fortitude, and it puts the beauty of marital love before us as something to be protected, defended, and sought.

Chastity continues into marriage. Chastity enlists husband and wife and all the world into an acknowledgment of the high honor and glory of marriage and the marriage bed.

The devil has different ideas. He knows that the blessing of intimacy is easily perverted. The devil takes desire and fans it into lust. He sends people in every wrong direction. The multitude of ways we've invented to break the Sixth Commandment is astonishing, and the list seems to be getting longer.

Many commentators have noted that we are living in a sexual revolution. We can trace the modern roots back a century. Technological advances in "birth control" disconnected the act of intimacy from the conception of children, or at least attempted this separation. (Abortion was a backup in case the technology failed.) Feminism shaped up as the move to give women the same "risk-free" access to sex that men have. The legalization of no-fault divorce meant that marriage was a temporary arrangement. The rise of the hook-up culture and the legalization of same-sex "marriage" are marks in the rising tide of our culture's pursuit of sexual pleasure.

All of this involves a reduction. No "liberated sexual act" is for pro-creation. All of these trends reduce our body to a tool—almost always pleasure for pleasure's sake (until addiction makes the act an obsession). This is a direct assault on the Lord's gift of sex—a cheap imitation, but one the devil uses to great effect.

First, as we discussed previously, the devil uses our desires to befriend us and to cause us to consider the Lord our enemy. Second, then, Christians are considered "prudes," "backward," even "repressive." The devil changes our vision to blur what is good, beautiful, and right.

Remember Adam and Eve in the garden. They looked on the forbidden fruit, and their vision was blurred. They did not see death. They did not see God's wrath. They did not see the unfolding years of horror. They saw that the tree was delightful and good for food. The same thing happened to King David when he saw Bathsheba bathing on the roof.

His sight was blurred. He couldn't see the violence and destruction that would unfold. He couldn't see the pain and death that would follow. He only saw Bathsheba, and his flesh took over.

The devil has blurred our cultural vision of intimacy. He has blurred our cultural vision of purity. Our pleasures are exalted, treasured as the highest good, even worshiped. Anything else, any suggestion that sex has a proper place, is blasphemy, a punishable offense. Any hint that intimacy ought to be shaped by God's commandment is a violent assault on pleasure.

The Christian is constantly tempted to join this revolution in a dozen different ways. The individual temptation to sexual immorality. The cultural pressure to redefine love and embrace tolerance. The weight of friendships, the sorrow of neighbors, the noise of media bring dishonor to marriage and the marriage bed. "Throw off the oppressive and binding command of God. Love and be free," the devil and the flesh preach.

All the while, the Christian sees God's gift of husband and wife and says, "This is very good."

Perhaps some of the intensity of sexual sin is explained by the unique gift of marriage and the unique danger of sexual immorality. No other sin has as profound an effect on the conscience. Paul notes the uniqueness of sexual sin.

> **Flee from sexual immorality. Every other sin a person commits is outside the body, but the sexually immoral person sins against his own body. Or do you not know that your body is a temple of the Holy Spirit within you, whom you have from God? You are not your own, for you were bought with a price. So glorify God in your body.**
>
> (1 Corinthians 6:18–20)

Flee is about as strong a word as you could use, and for good reason. Sexual immorality does damage. It damages the conscience, it damages the person, it damages the family, it damages the home and the church and the state. It is an assault on our humanity. It is an assault, for the

Christian, on the Gospel. "You are not your own. You were bought with a price." That price is the blood of Jesus.

A WORD FOR THE WOUNDED

No doubt, some of you reading these pages are casualties of the sexual revolution. For you, a word of hope. Jesus' death is for you. His suffering, His blood, His sacrifice is for you, to forgive you and to cleanse you.

The story of David and Bathsheba is both instructive and comforting, especially David's repentance (see 2 Samuel 11 and 12). David's repentance was not immediate. In fact, he covered up his sins of adultery and murder for more than a year, but the preaching of the prophet Nathan crushed him. David, at last, knew his sin and wickedness, and he begged the Lord for mercy. Psalm 51 was composed for the occasion. "Have mercy on me, O God, according to Your steadfast love; according to Your abundant mercy blot out my transgressions" (Psalm 51:1). The Lord had mercy. "The LORD also has put away your sin," Nathan comforted David. "You shall not die" (2 Samuel 12:13).

There were consequences for David's sin. His boy died. There was chaos in his family. His reign was marked with difficulty, rebellion, and all kinds of trouble. But David's sins were forgiven; he was right with God.

Jesus forgives sin, even the sexual sins that are so dangerous for the conscience. He washes us so that we are whiter than snow. "The blood of Jesus His Son cleanses us from all sin" (1 John 1:7).

The devil loves to tempt us to sin, and then he loves to rub our sin in our face, to make us wallow in our guilt and shame. Jesus forgives sin, your sin. It's why He died. He rescues you from guilt and sets you free in this life to rejoice in His light and peace.

THE MONEY ILLUSION

Money is the second overgrown weed, the temptation of our flesh that Jesus warns us about time and time again.

Consider these passages:

> See the man who would not make God his refuge, but trusted in the abundance of his riches and sought refuge in his own destruction! (PSALM 52:7)

> He who loves money will not be satisfied with money, nor he who loves wealth with his income; this also is vanity.
> (ECCLESIASTES 5:10)

Jesus takes up this warning and sounds the alarm on greed, covetousness, and trusting in wealth.

> No one can serve two masters, for either he will hate the one and love the other, or he will be devoted to the one and despise the other. You cannot serve God and money.
> (MATTHEW 6:24–25)

> Jesus looked around and said to His disciples, "How difficult it will be for those who have wealth to enter the kingdom of God!" And the disciples were amazed at His words. But Jesus said to them again, "Children, how difficult it is to enter the kingdom of God! It is easier for a camel to go through the eye of a needle than for a rich person to enter the kingdom of God." And they were exceedingly astonished, and said to Him, "Then who can be saved?"
> (MARK 10:23–26)

Here's another warning from Jesus:

> He said to them, "Take care, and be on your guard against all covetousness, for one's life does not consist in the abundance of his possessions." (LUKE 12:15)

Jesus then went on to tell the parable of the man who had a huge harvest. He pulled down his barns to build bigger barns to hold all his stuff.

> [This rich man] thought to himself . . . "Soul, you have ample goods laid up for many years; relax, eat, drink, be

merry." But God said to him, "Fool! This night your soul is required of you, and the things you have prepared, whose will they be?" So is the one who lays up treasure for himself and is not rich toward God. (LUKE 12:17–21)

The Bible tells us that the Pharisees, the chief opponents of Jesus, were lovers of money. Jesus rebukes them for it.

The Pharisees, who were lovers of money, heard all these things, and they ridiculed Him. And He said to them, "You are those who justify yourselves before men, but God knows your hearts. For what is exalted among men is an abomination in the sight of God." (LUKE 16:14–15)

Taking this altogether, we start to get a picture of the danger of the love of money.

Money tempts us with the illusion of security. We think that if we have it, we are safe, and if we don't have it, we are in danger. We should know better. There is a reason they print birds on money: to remind us that it flies away. "Do not toil to acquire wealth; be discerning enough to desist. When your eyes light on it, it is gone, for suddenly it sprouts wings, flying like an eagle toward heaven" (Proverbs 23:4–5).

The danger is that money becomes our god.

Martin Luther calls money the most common idol in the world.

Many a person thinks that he has God and everything in abundance when he has money and possessions. He trusts in them and boasts about them with such firmness and assurance as to care for no one. Such a person has a god by the name of "Mammon" (i.e., money and possessions), on which he sets all his heart. This is the most common idol on earth. He who has money and possessions feels secure and is joyful and undismayed as though he were sitting in the midst of Paradise. On the other hand, he who has no money doubts and is despondent, as though he knew of no God. For very few can be found who are of

good cheer and who neither mourn nor complain if they
lack Mammon. This care and desire for money sticks and
clings to our nature, right up to the grave. (LARGE CATECHISM,
FIRST COMMANDMENT, 5–9)

Like every false god, money wants us to put our trust in him, look
to him for all good, rely on him in times of trouble, fear and love him
above all else. Like all the old idols, money requires human sacrifice.
We can see it around us if we open our eyes. The Lord intends for us
to have stuff to take care of our families and bless our neighbors. But
most people don't have stuff; their stuff has them. They are caretakers
of their possessions. They are slaves to their riches.

Luther notices that you don't have to have money to worship it. This
idolatry is possible for the rich *and* the poor. The poor worry about how
to get money, and the rich worry about how to keep it.

The liturgy of the worship of money is worry.

Jesus condemns it. We are not authorized to worry. That's the kind
of stuff the pagans do.

Therefore do not be anxious, saying, "What shall we
eat?" or "What shall we drink?" or "What shall we wear?"
For the Gentiles seek after all these things, and your heavenly Father knows that you need them all. But seek first
the kingdom of God and His righteousness, and all these
things will be added to you. (MATTHEW 6:31–33)

This does not mean that we should not work. This does not mean
that we do not make money and spend money. Working and worrying
are two different things. We use money. We are careful that our money
does not use us. It is the *love* of money that is the root of all kinds of
evil (see 1 Timothy 6:10).

That text captures what we are getting after in this section.

But godliness with contentment is great gain, for we
brought nothing into the world, and we cannot take anything out of the world. But if we have food and clothing,

with these we will be content. But those who desire to be rich fall into temptation, into a snare, into many senseless and harmful desires that plunge people into ruin and destruction. For the love of money is a root of all kinds of evils. It is through this craving that some have wandered away from the faith and pierced themselves with many pangs. But as for you, O man of God, flee these things. Pursue righteousness, godliness, faith, love, steadfastness, gentleness. (1 TIMOTHY 6:6–11)

Notice how Paul highlights that the danger is in the desire: those who "desire to be rich," the "love of money," through "this craving . . . some have wandered" from the faith. Our sinful flesh is greedy and discontented.

The worship of money, at last, lets us trust in ourselves. If we have enough money, we become our own god and our own savior. Jesus has different plans.

For you know the grace of our Lord Jesus Christ, that though He was rich, yet for your sake He became poor, so that you by His poverty might become rich. (2 CORINTHIANS 8:9)

Jesus knows that we are tempted by the false god of money, that our flesh loves the idol mammon, but He saves us from this, knowing that the end of these things is destruction.

Our treasure is in heaven. Our riches are the righteousness of Christ. Our inheritance of eternal life is secure.

22

Sanctification Is a Lot of Little Deaths

Those who belong to Christ Jesus have crucified the flesh with its passions and desires.

(GALATIANS 5:24)

What are we supposed to do with our sinful flesh? What are we supposed to do with these sinful desires that push us away from God and His goodness?

We are at war with our sinful flesh. Paul says it this way:

I say, walk by the Spirit, and you will not gratify the desires of the flesh. For the desires of the flesh are against the Spirit, and the desires of the Spirit are against the flesh, for these are opposed to each other, to keep you from doing the things you want to do. (GALATIANS 5:16–17)

Flesh and Spirit, fighting inside us. "Beloved, I urge you as sojourners and exiles to abstain from the passions of the flesh, which wage war against your soul" (1 Peter 2:11). This fight lasts as long as we are alive (see Romans 7:13–25).

We can think of our flesh as a fire. If we feed it and put fuel on it, it grows hotter. If, on the other hand, we stamp it down, douse it with water, and take fuel away, it diminishes. If you sow to the flesh, you reap corruption (see Galatians 6:8).

Consider Paul's instructions to the Romans: "But put on the Lord Jesus Christ, and make no provision for the flesh, to gratify its desires" (Romans 13:14).

The old theologians called this "mortification"—putting the flesh to death. We'll let Martin Luther walk us through this.

In 1521, Luther wrote an important little book called *The Freedom of a Christian*. In it, he put forth the great Reformation teaching of justification by grace through faith, that we are saved completely apart from our works and efforts.

> **Wherefore it ought to be the first concern of every Christian to lay aside all confidence in works and increasingly to strengthen faith alone and through faith to grow in the knowledge, not of works, but of Christ Jesus, who suffered and rose for him, as Peter teaches in the last chapter of his first Epistle (1 Peter 5:10). No other work makes a Christian.** (AE 31:347)

There is, though, a place for Christian works. The inner man is free and holy by faith. The outward man lives before his neighbor by his works. These works begin with mortification, reining in the sinful flesh.

> **Although, as I have said, a man is abundantly and sufficiently justified by faith inwardly, in his spirit, and so has all that he needs, except insofar as this faith and these riches must grow from day to day even to the future life; yet he remains in this mortal life on earth. In this life he must control his own body and have dealings with men. Here the works begin; here a man cannot enjoy leisure; here he must indeed take care to discipline his body by fastings, watchings, labors, and other reasonable discipline and to subject it to the Spirit so that it will obey and**

conform to the inner man and faith and not revolt against faith and hinder the inner man, as it is the nature of the body to do if it is not held in check. The inner man, who by faith is created in the image of God, is both joyful and happy because of Christ in whom so many benefits are conferred upon him; and therefore it is his one occupation to serve God joyfully and without thought of gain, in love that is not constrained. (AE 31:358–59)

Notice the language Luther uses. The "body" refers to the sinful flesh. The "inner man, who by faith is created in the image of God" is the Christian new man, what St. Paul calls the "Spirit." The body must be subject to "reasonable discipline" so that it remains subject to the Spirit and doesn't run amuck.

Luther lists "fastings, watchings, and labors" as three of these disciplines that Christians practice to discipline the flesh, a list he draws from 2 Corinthians 6:

As servants of God we commend ourselves in every way: by great endurance, in afflictions, hardships, calamities, beatings, imprisonments, riots, *labors, sleepless nights, hunger*; by purity, knowledge, patience, kindness, the Holy Spirit, genuine love. (vv. 4–6)

Fasting is not eating. Watching is not sleeping, staying awake to pray. Labors are difficult works that serve the neighbor. All three involve not giving the flesh what it wants.

Our stomachs grumble at us, telling us that we are hungry and need food. When we fast, we say to our stomachs, "You're not in charge here." Our bodies get tired, telling us to get some sleep. When we stay awake to watch and pray, we are telling our flesh, "You're not the boss." Our flesh loves to take it easy. When we labor, when we use our bodies and our work to bless our neighbor, we deny ourselves.

There is a "training" aspect of this discipline. Paul reminds us that it is by God's grace that we are trained to renounce worldly passions.

> For the grace of God has appeared, bringing salvation for all people, training us to renounce ungodliness and worldly passions, and to live self-controlled, upright, and godly lives in the present age, waiting for our blessed hope, the appearing of the glory of our great God and Savior Jesus Christ, who gave Himself for us to redeem us from all lawlessness and to purify for Himself a people for His own possession who are zealous for good works. (Titus 2:11–14)

Luther remembers the extreme discipline of the monastery. He used to whip himself, expose himself to the cold, go weeks without food, and treat his body brutally in his search for perfection. That is not what he is talking about. Luther reminds us that this is a "reasonable discipline," measured. We are not supposed to kill ourselves. But neither are we to seek a life of indulgence and ease.

Most often, we do not need to look for troubles. The Lord will give them to us. We considered above the Lord's work in suffering. We remember how Peter noted that suffering weakens our sinful desires.

> Since therefore Christ suffered in the flesh, arm yourselves with the same way of thinking, for whoever has suffered in the flesh has ceased from sin, so as to live for the rest of the time in the flesh no longer for human passions but for the will of God. (1 Peter 4:1–2)

Luther notes that the inner man is free and happy, delighting in the benefits of Christ, and ready to love and serve his neighbor. The inner man is interested in managing the flesh so that it doesn't stand in the way of love.

Luther continues:

> While he is doing this, behold, he meets a contrary will in his own flesh which strives to serve the world and seeks its own advantage. This the spirit of faith cannot tolerate, but with joyful zeal it attempts to put the body under control and hold it in check, as Paul says in Romans 7 [:22–23],

"For I delight in the law of God, in my inmost self, but I see in my members another law at war with the law of my mind and making me captive to the law of sin," and in another place, "But I pommel my body and subdue it, lest after preaching to others I myself should be disqualified" [1 Corinthians 9:27], and in Galatians [5:24], "And those who belong to Christ Jesus have crucified the flesh with its passions and desires." (AE 31:359)

While our inner man, the spirit, goes about the business of loving God and neighbor, it finds another will, a contrary will, a will drawn to the world and seeking after its own desires. The spirit cannot abide this contrary will. It fights back, subdues it, and, at last, crucifies the flesh. The flesh, at last, must be put off and put to death.

Put off your old self, which belongs to your former manner of life and is corrupt through deceitful desires, and . . . be renewed in the spirit of your minds, and . . . put on the new self, created after the likeness of God in true righteousness and holiness. (EPHESIANS 4:22–24; SEE ALSO 1 PETER 2:11–12)

Put to death therefore what is earthly in you: sexual immorality, impurity, passion, evil desire, and covetousness, which is idolatry. On account of these the wrath of God is coming. In these you too once walked, when you were living in them. But now you must put them all away: anger, wrath, malice, slander, and obscene talk from your mouth. Do not lie to one another, seeing that you have put off the old self with its practices and have put on the new self, which is being renewed in knowledge after the image of its creator. (COLOSSIANS 3:5–10)

There is a difference in the life of an unbeliever and a Christian. Paul notes that we once walked according to the desires of the flesh, we fed our appetites, and we were driven by our passions, but no longer (see also Ephesians 2:3). These things are put away, put to death. We wear the new self, which is constantly "renewed in knowledge" and the image of our Creator.

Notice that Paul here talks about the restoration of what was lost in the garden. The "image of [the] creator" (Colossians 3:10) and the "likeness of God" (Ephesians 4:24) is being restored as the sinful flesh is put off, as the old man is laid aside, and as we put on Christ.

This putting on Christ is what happens in our Baptism (Galatians 3:27) and continues in our life of repentance. The two parts of repentance are a drowning of the flesh and the coming forth of the new man (see also Romans 6:2–4).

The language of putting to death the flesh is all over the Bible.

> **Those who belong to Christ Jesus have crucified the flesh with its passions and desires.** (GALATIANS 5:24)

> **We know that our old self was crucified with Him in order that the body of sin might be brought to nothing, so that we would no longer be enslaved to sin. For one who has died has been set free from sin.** (ROMANS 6:6–7)

Notice how this death of the flesh sets us free. We are no longer slaves to our passions and lusts.

> **So then, brothers, we are debtors, not to the flesh, to live according to the flesh. For if you live according to the flesh you will die, but if by the Spirit you put to death the deeds of the body, you will live. For all who are led by the Spirit of God are sons of God.** (ROMANS 8:12–14)

Luther wants to make sure we have this work of mortification in the proper theological place. We are not crucifying our flesh to be justified before God.

> **In doing these works, however, we must not think that a man is justified before God by them, for faith, which alone is righteousness before God, cannot endure that erroneous opinion. We must, however, realize that these works**

reduce the body to subjection and purify it of its evil lusts, and our whole purpose is to be directed only toward the driving out of lusts. Since by faith the soul is cleansed and made to love God, it desires that all things, and especially its own body, shall be purified so that all things may join with it in loving and praising God. Hence a man cannot be idle, for the need of his body drives him and he is compelled to do many good works to reduce it to subjection. Nevertheless the works themselves do not justify him before God, but he does the works out of spontaneous love in obedience to God and considers nothing except the approval of God, whom he would most scrupulously obey in all things. (AE 31:359)

We work to "drive out lusts," to "reduce the body to subjection," to control our bodies so that they would be instruments of righteousness.

Our flesh drives and draws us to sin and death, but Christ has triumphed over the world, the devil, and even our own sinful flesh. Paul unfolds this doctrine with a note of triumph and joy.

For if we have been united with Him in a death like His [through Baptism], we shall certainly be united with Him in a resurrection like His. We know that our old self was crucified with Him in order that the body of sin might be brought to nothing, so that we would no longer be enslaved to sin. For one who has died has been set free from sin. Now if we have died with Christ, we believe that we will also live with Him. We know that Christ, being raised from the dead, will never die again; death no longer has dominion over Him. For the death He died He died to sin, once for all, but the life He lives He lives to God. So you also must consider yourselves dead to sin and alive to God in Christ Jesus. (Romans 6:5–11)

Look at the promises Paul has given us in these verses. We are united with Christ in a death like His. We will be raised with Him. Our flesh

PART 4 | IN THE WEEDS

was crucified with Him. The body of sin (that is, our sinful flesh) is brought to nothing. We are no longer enslaved to sin. Death no longer has dominion over Christ or over us. We are dead to sin. We are alive to Christ. And we know it!

> I have been crucified with Christ. It is no longer I who live, but Christ who lives in me. And the life I now live in the flesh I live by faith in the Son of God, who loved me and gave Himself for me. (GALATIANS 2:20)

23

True Freedom and the Full Life

*The thief comes only to steal and kill
and destroy. I came that they may have
life and have it abundantly.*

(JOHN 10:10)

The devil lies through our flesh. He promises the good life, freedom, and satisfaction when the sinful desires of our flesh are fulfilled. The devil puts the path of pleasure before us and says, "This is the road of freedom leading to life."

The devil hides what the Bible reveals: the desires of the flesh are a bondage leading to death. "Everyone who practices sin is a slave to sin" (John 8:34). "For the end of those things is death" (Romans 6:21). Remember the anatomy of sin from James (1:15): desire is conceived and gives birth to sin, and when it is grown, it brings forth death.

Our sinful desires are bad and dangerous, but this does not mean that we are to have no desire at all. In fact, the Bible commands us to want and desire, but this is a desire for the right things. We desire the Lord's kindness. We delight in His Word. We rejoice in His doctrine. We want things to go well with our neighbor. We treasure our family and friends. We find joy in the gifts of God.

God does not intend that we live an empty, desireless existence. Jesus came to give us a full and abundant life, a life rich in His blessings.

Paul contrasts the desires of the flesh with the fruit of the Spirit. This text really summarizes all that we have been discussing:

> But I say, walk by the Spirit, and you will not gratify the desires of the flesh. For the desires of the flesh are against the Spirit, and the desires of the Spirit are against the flesh, for these are opposed to each other, to keep you from doing the things you want to do. But if you are led by the Spirit, you are not under the law. Now the works of the flesh are evident: sexual immorality, impurity, sensuality, idolatry, sorcery, enmity, strife, jealousy, fits of anger, rivalries, dissensions, divisions, envy, drunkenness, orgies, and things like these. I warn you, as I warned you before, that those who do such things will not inherit the kingdom of God. But the fruit of the Spirit is love, joy, peace, patience, kindness, goodness, faithfulness, gentleness, self-control; against such things there is no law. And those who belong to Christ Jesus have crucified the flesh with its passions and desires. (GALATIANS 5:16–24)

Not only does the Lord put to death the desires of the flesh, but He also brings about life, an abundance of the fruits of the Spirit.

I think the abundant life that the Lord has for us is seen most clearly in the petitions of the Lord's Prayer. This prayer is an inventory of the gifts and riches that the Lord wants for us.

I remember in some biology class learning what human beings need for life: air, water, eventually food, and shelter. This is what is needed for life, for physical life, but this is a very small and reduced view of life. Jesus wants us to have more, to want more, to desire more, and to be satisfied with more. "Open your mouth wide," the Lord says to us, "and I will fill it" (Psalm 81:10).

In the Lord's Prayer, Jesus is expanding and reshaping our spiritual desires. It is as if He is saying, "Here are the things you need, the things you should want, and the things that I want to give you." How wonderful!

We need the Lord, His name and Word: "Hallowed by Thy name."

We need His kingdom, His gracious rule in our midst by His Holy Spirit: "Thy kingdom come."

We need His gracious will to be done. We need His help fighting off the devil, the world, and even our own sinful desires: "Thy will be done."

We need a bite to eat, a place to live, things to keep our bodies alive: "Give us this day our daily bread."

We need the blood of Jesus, His atoning sacrifice, His imputed righteousness: "Forgive us."

We need His help curbing our flesh. We need His wisdom: "Lead us not into temptation."

We need to die and go to heaven. We need the resurrection of the body and life everlasting: "Deliver us from evil."

This is the Lord's outline of right desires. This is Jesus' official and authorized list of good things we should want. What a list! How rich we are in Christ! What treasures we have in His name! Look at the love the Lord has lavished on us, that we should be called His children, that we should call Him our Father, that we should be the heirs of His name and kingdom.

The devil deceived Adam and Eve into thinking that the fruit would give them more. "If you eat it, you will be wise, you will know good and evil." But there was no wisdom there, only foolishness. Adam and Eve already knew what was good—everything was good. They were very good. But after they ate the fruit, they knew evil. This was not more, it was less. They were less. They knew the good that was lost and the evil that was brought about.

The devil only steals. He only destroys. He only diminishes. Still.

He tempts our flesh to have more—more fun, more pleasure, more riches, more leisure, more whatever—but it is an empty more, a vain abundance, fleeting at best. The desires of the flesh are corrosive and destructive.

In the parable of the sower, the weeds choked the good plants. It is no accident that Jesus uses this language. The pleasures of this life are strangling. They eat away at what is good. They pry us away from what is holy. They tickle us toward a whimpering death. The color is slowly drained; the sap drips out of life until there is nothing left. We feast on rot and ask for more.

Jesus has the true "more." He *is* the true abundance. He is life so abundant that it never ends. True pleasure, true joy, and true contentment are found in Him.

> Delight yourself in the Lord, and He will give you the desires of your heart. (Psalm 37:4)

GOOD

DIRT

ST. AGATHA: MARTYR. HERO.
AD 251. Sicily.

Agatha was a young woman, fifteen years old, who took a vow of virginity. She committed herself to study of the Scriptures and prayer. This was during the persecution of Decius (250–53).

This was a great disappointment to Quintianus, who was determined to marry her. He was a judge, so he, knowing she was illegally a Christian, brought her into his court, offering her the option of marriage or torture.

She prayed, "Jesus Christ, Lord of all, You see my heart, You know my desires. Possess all that I am. I am Your sheep; make me worthy to overcome the devil." Weeping and praying for courage, she confessed her faith.

Quintianus sentenced her to a month in a brothel where she was abused and assaulted. He called for her again, and when she still confessed her faith, she was tortured, stretched on the rack, torn with iron hooks, whipped, and burned with torches. She was sentenced to burning at the stake, but an earthquake saved her.

Agatha skipped joyfully to her execution, like she was going to a feast or a dance. She laughed and rejoiced. She said,

Unless you cause my body to be broken by your executioner, my soul will not be able to enter paradise bearing the Victor's palm, even as a grain of wheat, unless it is stripped of its husk and harshly beaten on the threshing floor, is not gathered into the barn. (AE 42:160)

Agatha: Martyr. Hero.
We'll meet in the resurrection.

24

Unless the Seed Falls to the Ground and Dies

*Truly, truly, I say to you, unless a grain
of wheat falls into the earth and dies, it remains
alone; but if it dies, it bears much fruit.*

(JOHN 12:24)

Jesus ends the parable of the sower with hope.

> Other seeds fell on good soil and produced grain, some
> a hundredfold, some sixty, some thirty. He who has ears,
> let him hear. (MATTHEW 13:8–9)

What does it mean to be the good soil? Jesus explains:

> As for what was sown on good soil, this is the one who
> hears the word and understands it. He indeed bears fruit
> and yields, in one case a hundredfold, in another sixty, and
> in another thirty. (MATTHEW 13:23)

Hearing the Word. Understanding the Word. That's it.

This seed does not grow because the dirt possesses some sort of super-spiritual fertilizer. This plant does not survive because of the great holiness of the dirt. The power is in the Word.

The Word of God creates faith. The Word of God sustains and strengthens our faith. The Word of God beats back the devil. The Word of God gives us patience to suffer. The Word of God fights against our flesh. The Word of God preserves us in the faith, produces the fruit of love, and prepares us for the untold bliss of the life to come.

The Word, the Word, the Word.

There is no secret to spiritual warfare. There is no fast track to Christian maturity. We finish where we start: the kindness of God promised to us in the humble preached Word.

When we take up the Scriptures, we find that Jesus is already fighting the devil. When we turn to God's Word, we find our Lord already preparing us to suffer. When we take up the Bible, we find our flesh being subdued. The Lord fights for us, and He plans to finish what He started.

25

Jesus Is Our Champion

The LORD of hosts is with us;
The God of Jacob is our fortress.

(PSALM 46:11)

So much talk of spiritual warfare and Christian discipline points to the Christian. We are taking up arms. We are marching out to battle. We are doing our part.

There is something to this. We are enlisted in the Lord's work. We are to believe, love, pray, and fight against the devil. But we must remember that Jesus is our Champion. He is the One who first fights for us. His victory is our hope, His strength is our shield.

Psalm 46 captures this for us wonderfully. The picture is of a city under attack. The city is fortified, a refuge for all who live in it, but it is surrounded by such great and mighty foes that the earth is shaking, the mountains are falling over, the ocean is trembling.

The first stanza of the song tells us to look inside this city. God is there! We will be safe. No matter what is happening outside the city walls, we are protected. There is nothing to fear.

> **God is our refuge and strength,**
> **a very present help in trouble.**
> **Therefore we will not fear though the earth gives way,**

> though the mountains be moved into the heart of the sea,
> though its waters roar and foam,
> though the mountains tremble at its swelling.
> (PSALM 46:1–3)

There is a river in this fortress, that is, the Holy Spirit and the Word of God. We are well provided for. God, who is with us, only needs to say the Word, and all His enemies will come to nothing.

> There is a river whose streams make glad the city of God,
> the holy habitation of the Most High.
> God is in the midst of her; she shall not be moved;
> God will help her when morning dawns.
> The nations rage, the kingdoms totter;
> He utters His voice, the earth melts. (PSALM 46:4–6)

Then comes the refrain, a shout of confidence:

> The LORD of hosts is with us;
> the God of Jacob is our fortress. (PSALM 46:7)

In the second stanza, we are summoned to the city walls to see what is happening outside, to see the battle. We see all the enemies gathered around us, but then, through the gate goes our Champion. "Ask ye, Who is this? Jesus Christ it is." He goes forth to scatter the enemies, to break the bow and shatter the spear. He makes an end of war by making an end of His enemies, your enemies.

> Come, behold the works of the LORD,
> how He has brought desolations on the earth.
> He makes wars cease to the end of the earth;
> He breaks the bow and shatters the spear;
> He burns the chariots with fire. (PSALM 46:8–9)

You are watching as He fights for you. As He overthrows all Your enemies, He looks back at you and says,

> "Be still, and know that I am God.

I will be exalted among the nations,
I will be exalted in the earth!" (PSALM 46:10)

"You stay there," the Lord says, "I've got this. I will be exalted. I will be lifted up. I will be crucified. I will triumph over sin. I will break the power of death. I will crush the devil. I will be the Savior, your Savior." His victory is your victory.

Our confidence is not in ourselves but in the Lord Jesus, who takes up the fight for us. We tremble not, we fear no ill. The devil, the world, and the flesh cannot overpower Him. He is our Champion.

The LORD of hosts is with us;
the God of Jacob is our fortress. (PSALM 46:11)

26

The Difficulty of Being Paul's Enemy

I have learned in whatever situation I am to be content.

(PHILIPPIANS 4:11)

Imagine, for a moment, that you are the enemy of St. Paul. You hate him. You hate his preaching and teaching. You hate his friends. You hate his work. You hate the way he looks. Everything about him makes you crazy. You want him to suffer.

You get your friends together. "I hate this Paul," you say. "We need to get him. Let's kill him."

They all nod in agreement. Your friends are a bunch of thugs. But one of them says, "I saw a letter that Paul wrote to Philippi, and in it he said, 'For me, to die is gain.'"

"We don't want that," you say, frustrated. "Well, let's cause him to suffer. Let's throw him in prison and torture him."

"Yes!" they all shout, except for another friend who says, "I was reading a little part of a letter he sent to Rome. He wrote, 'Not only that, but we rejoice in our sufferings, knowing that suffering produces endurance,' and some other nonsense."

"Yeah," said the first guy, "he said something like that in the letter I read, about being granted the gift of suffering."

"Just great," you say with frustration. "What are we going to do? Let him live?"

"Well," says your friend, "he also said in his letter, 'For me, to live is Christ.'"

There's nothing you can do to Paul!

He rejoices in death. He rejoices in life. He rejoices in suffering. He is content with plenty. He is content with little. His treasure is Christ, and this can't be taken from him.

Imagine the frustration of being his enemy. Imagine the frustration of being the devil and wanting to destroy Paul. There's nothing you can do to him. How is this possible? What does Paul know that makes him so unassailable?

Nothing more than us. Paul had the Gospel. You have the Gospel. Paul had the promise that Christ died for him. You have that same promise. Paul had the blood of Jesus. You have that some blood. Paul had the Word of God. You have that same Word, "the implanted word, which is able to save your souls" (James 1:21). Paul had Jesus. Or better: Jesus had Paul, and Jesus has you.

Imagine, then, the frustration of your enemies. Imagine the frustration of the devil who hates you. You are learning to be content in all things. For you, to live is Christ and to die is gain. All things are working together for your good, in suffering and hardship, in life and death.

Nothing, it turns out, can separate us from the love of Christ: not tribulation, not distress, not persecution, not famine, not nakedness, not danger, not the sword. It is true, we are being assaulted and killed all day long. We are marked like sheep to be slaughtered, but "in all these things we are more than conquerors through Him who loved us" (Romans 8:33–37).

Paul has this confidence not only for himself but also for us.

For I am sure that neither death nor life, nor angels nor rulers, nor things present nor things to come, nor powers, nor height nor depth, nor anything else in all creation, will be able to separate us from the love of God in Christ Jesus our Lord. (ROMANS 8:38–39)

27

Encouragement for the Weary

Therefore, since we are surrounded by so great
a cloud of witnesses, let us also lay aside every
weight, and sin which clings so closely, and let us
run with endurance the race that is set before us,
looking to Jesus, the founder and perfecter of
our faith, who for the joy that was set before Him
endured the cross, despising the shame, and is
seated at the right hand of the throne of God.

(HEBREWS 12:1–2)

Imagine yourself running a race. It's a marathon, or longer, one of those races that goes on and on. You pass a few people, but mostly everyone has passed you. You are hungry and tired, your tongue is glued to the roof of your mouth, and your lungs feel like they are stuffed with flaming cotton. You try to sing and pray through the pain, and it seems like this race will never end.

This is one of those races that ends in the stadium, but it seems like you are nowhere close to the finish. Every time you climb over a little hill, all you see are more hills, more track, more running. Your feet drag. Your heart pounds. Your mind thinks only of quitting, of lying down on the side of the road.

But then you hear a sound, faint, in the distance—people cheering. And as you come along, you see the stadium, the track, and the end of the race. The sound gets louder, and you think you hear a familiar voice. You do! As you get closer, you see the faces of the people in the stands, and you recognize them, and they see you. Their faces light up when they recognize you, and they cheer even louder.

This is the picture given to us in Hebrews 12. "Since we are surrounded by so great a cloud of witnesses, let us also lay aside every weight, and sin which clings so closely, and let us run with endurance the race that is set before us."

You turn the corner into the stadium and there, in the front row, are your grandparents, cheering you on. Your parents, the friends and family who have died before you. They are yelling, encouraging, "You can make it."

Suddenly your legs are not so heavy.

You see next to them others whom you recognize. There is Martin Luther, Martin Chemnitz, the crowd of faithful reformers, and they are cheering for you as well. "Stay strong!" they say. "You are almost to the end."

You begin to forget your pain, your hunger, and your thirst.

Further along in the stadium are the Church Fathers, the martyrs, the apostles. There is Peter. "Christ also suffered," he says. "Run with joy." There is Paul. "Keep the faith," he yells to you. There are Thomas and Matthew, and James and John, all pushing you on.

You begin to run faster.

You see Jeremiah and Isaiah, comforting you, and it seems as if your feet have grown wings. There is King David. "Don't grow weary!" There is Joshua. "Be strong and courageous!" he shouts. There are Moses and Aaron, Joseph and Judah, Abraham and Sarah, and Noah with his family, and Abel, and Adam and Eve. "We made it. We finished. You can too!" Can you imagine it!

There are the heroes, those who have finished the race, who kept the faith. The great cloud of finishers.

You are running with purpose now, and you make the last turn. You see the finish line. There, standing at the end, is Jesus. His arms are stretched out. He is waiting for you. You see the scars in His hands. His eyes are fixed on you. He smiles. "A little further," He says, "just a little while. A few more steps." You are sprinting now. You throw off anything that is slowing you down. Weariness is forgotten. You can't hear the crowd anymore. Hope is set before you. Hearts are brave again, and arms are strong.

Therefore, since we are surrounded by so great a cloud of witnesses, let us also lay aside every weight, and sin which clings so closely, and let us run with endurance the race that is set before us, looking to Jesus, the founder and perfecter of our faith, who for the joy that was set before Him endured the cross, despising the shame, and is seated at the right hand of the throne of God. (HEBREWS 12:1–2)

Jesus is the beginning, and Jesus is the end. He is the source and the goal, the start and the finish. He is at the Father's right hand, and you will be there soon. And in the meantime, while we labor here below, Jesus waits. He prays for you. He prepares a place for you. He finishes the work that He began in you, and He will bring it to completion in His time.

We are not seeking to have a martyr's faith in a faithless world. We are seeking Jesus, striving for Him, grasping to take hold of His eternal life, knowing that He has already taken hold of us. He is our finish line, and soon we will reach Him.

Amen.

Epilogue

Luther on the Joy and Gladness of the Martyrs as They Go to the Death

With joy and gladness they are led along as they enter the palace of the King.

[PSALM 45:15]

Change the tense from the future to the present. He is sketching how the church and the people of God are led into the palace, to Christ Himself, as if to a dance and royal banquet. Therefore here, too, spiritual eyes are required, such as Saint Agatha had. When they were taken off to torture on account of their confession of Christ, she said they were being led to the dance and sumptuous feasts. So the church is exposed to all misfortunes and torments, and individual Christians are either thrown into prison or overwhelmed by sorrow, temptations, and martyrdom. Yet they suffer all these things with a joyous conscience, because the Holy Spirit is with them, making them despise the wrath and fury of the world and the devil with all his terrors, so that they even enter into danger with joy. How is it that Christians remain steadfast in so many temptations, tortures within and without, and still do not deny Christ? Because they know they are in the service of this King and are being led to Him in splendor. So I, too, could not make even one sermon in public if I were not encouraged by such promises that Christ lives and is our Lord. This brings forth a certain confidence, so that we can think this way: "If it is true that Christ is our Lord and King, then, whether we are killed or despoiled, you may still be joyful and unshaken in your mind." This is the allegorical dance about which the prophet speaks here, in which there is a joy that is neither natural nor carnal, but supernatural and spiritual, *overcoming the fears of death and despising the madness of hell and of Satan and his members*. The church should be instructed by faith; that is the golden garment. Then it must be adorned with love and patience, "that it may glory in tribulation" (Romans 5:3). Then, if anyone undergoes persecution for the sake of the Word, he may say: "Quite right. I have sought this by my preaching, that I might excite the world and Satan against me. But I will not quit on this account." So this dance will be danced correctly. (AE 12:295–96)